Please return/renew this item by the last date shown on this label, or on your self-service receipt.

To renew this item, visit **www.librarieswest.org.uk** or contact your library.

Your Borrower number and PIN are required.

A JOB WITH BITE

PETER CHAPLIN

SilverWood

Published in 2016 by SilverWood Books

SilverWood Books Ltd
14 Small Street, Bristol, BS1 1DE, United Kingdom
www.silverwoodbooks.co.uk

ISBN 978-1-78132-525-4

British Library Cataloguing in Publication Data
A CIP catalogue record for this book is available from
the British Library

Page design and typesetting by SilverWood Books
Printed by Imprint Digital on responsibly sourced paper

Avon & Somerset Dog Section 1978–98
Cops and Robbers for Grown-Ups
We worked hard; we played hard!
It really was
A Job with Bite

CONTENTS

INTRODUCTION

I am a Bristolian born and bred, and for the past fifty years I have lived on the Lockleaze council estate in North Bristol.

From 1970 until 1998 I was in the police service in the south west of England. For twenty of those twenty-eight years, I was a police dog handler. Over those twenty years, I arrested over five hundred criminals with the help of various canine partners. I kept a diary of each and every arrest, and although I have been retired for seventeen years, I recently found my diary in my loft, and decided to write my story, *A Job with Bite*.

Of my many dogs, the one that stands head and shoulders above the rest is Major. Major is the reason for this book – quite simply, he was a legend. Not because he was mine, but because he *was!*

In his five years of outstanding service, he bit thirty-four people – nineteen were criminals, seven were serving police officers, and eight were totally innocent members of the public, who unfortunately were in the wrong place at the wrong time.

Without Major, this book would be pointless. All of my other dogs were simply average. My skills as a dog trainer were quite limited, but what I lacked in natural talent I made up for with effort and sheer enthusiasm. I was a very good and keen handler, and together with Major we made a truly phenomenal team.

Major's story just had to be written! Perhaps once in a generation a dog of this type comes along. If there had been an SAS unit for dogs, believe me, Major would have been in it. There are simply not enough adjectives to describe how good this dog was.

This book has been in my mind since Major's demise in 1984. It has been seventeen years in the thinking and over one year in the writing. There are anecdotes from former officers, both witnesses and victims of Major's escapades.

To all of you that have bought this book and are reading it: a big thank-you.

To recollect totally accurately every incident from over thirty years ago has been an impossibility. With the aid of my 'dog arrests' diary I have been able to remember quite a number of incidents. However, there were occasions where I simply went along with the comments in the diary, as I could not totally recall every single event.

The comments and opinions in this book are mine and mine alone. As I said very clearly from the beginning, I was no great shakes as a dog trainer, and never claimed to be; it's just that I was lucky enough to have one particular unique canine partner that enabled me to be as successful as I was.

A dog is a pack animal, and they all want to be Top Dog. As a police dog that is not possible as the handler has to be Top Dog. I was once told this two-word description as to why a police dog complies with its handler's commands: RESPECTFUL FEAR. Respectful fear of the Top Dog!

With regard to the technical facts and figures concerning a dog's senses (hearing, sight and smell), I have been quite general in my novice explanations. I am certainly no veterinary academic and I do not have a deep understanding and knowledge of such involved subjects.

I have been totally honest (warts and all), and I am very sorry if I have offended anyone, as this was never my intention. Law enforcement officers globally will acknowledge and understand that on occasion the only way to deal with death, tragedy and sometimes the simply horrific is to not take things to heart, and not become emotionally involved. Sometimes what outsiders would consider a light-hearted approach to certain events is the only way to cope, and to not run the risk of becoming traumatised by what you witness to the extent that you end up in a spiral of depression. Flippancy or disrespect was never on my agenda.

To those I have not included (Firksy, Fred Collins, Ted Jones, Bob Lavis and Roy Jones) – I am sorry. Let me know and I will do my best to include you in Book 2.

One final mention to colleagues that I worked with and have sadly passed away. Some are mentioned in my book and some are not; however, these guys were part of a small, special team whose camaraderie and commitment to a living piece of equipment would probably only be appreciated and understood by fellow dog people worldwide. I would like to remember Bob Williams, Dick Burton, Bob Lonsdale, Pete Richards, Pat Long, Bob Forsyth, Paul Delancey, Steve Wilkinson, Brian Langley, Trevor Smith, Dick Cheetham, Mike Whiting, Martin Hillier, Alan King, and two guys who were before my time but were absolute legends, Derek Johnson and Alan Matthews.

God bless,
Pete, 2016

WHILST GROWING UP, MUM SAID, "NO DOGS ALLOWED!"

Southmead Hospital, Bristol
11.45pm, Sunday 5th April 1953 (Easter Sunday)

This is where the whole story began.

Peter Jesse Chaplin came into the world weighing 5lb 12 oz. My mum, Pauline Joyce Chaplin, was delighted. My dad, Lionel Jesse Chaplin, was over the moon. My mum had managed to squeeze me out a full fifteen minutes before the end of the tax year. Financially, this meant a tax rebate of around £6.10s (a veritable fortune in those days) to my dad. My dad was an agent for a hire purchase company, and my mum was a housewife.

We lived in a very small terraced house at 12 Hemmings Parade, Lawrence Hill, Bristol. This is where I spent the first eleven years of my life. Mum had a miscarriage in 1956 and was told that due to gynaecological issues she would not be able to have any more children.

My schools were Russell Town Avenue Infants, Avonvale Junior School, and then Brislington Comprehensive. This was up until 1964 when Bristol City Council compulsorily purchased our house and we moved, along with other neighbours, to a new council development at Morris Road, Lockleaze in Bristol. I had no option but to change schools, and I ended up going to Monks Park School on Gloucester Road.

During those first eleven years I obviously had no knowledge of the 'infertile state' of my mum. I would constantly nag and badger both Mum and Dad for a brother or sister (preferably a brother), but to no avail. At birthdays and Christmas, I would ask for a sibling, but nothing. Then one year, when I was about eight years old, I thought, why not have a dog? Surely that's the next best thing to a brother? This was a great idea to me, and the answer to my life of loneliness.

My mum was a working-class girl from Anstey Street in Easton. However, she was extremely house-proud and kept our little terraced house in Hemmings Parade like a palace. Upon hearing my request for a puppy, the short, sharp and loud reply came: "We are not having a dog!" As the years went by and no brother or sister arrived, that dreadful phrase, "We are not having a dog" was frequently repeated.

I was now in the first year of senior school at Monks Park. Despite being an only child I had the knack of getting on with people, and it wasn't long before I had quite a large circle of friends. I can honestly say that I enjoyed school very much. I am a reasonably intelligent guy – it's just that I am lazy. The exception to this is when I really want something, and then I go all out to achieve my goal (as with my application and interview to become a dog handler many years later). I had some very good mates at school. Sport was special to me, and I also enjoyed the debating society (perhaps that's where my gift of the gab began to develop).

In our school, there were eight class grades. The first three were classed as the grammar stream, doing O Levels, and classes 4, 5, 6, 7 and 8 were the CSE classes for children with lesser abilities. I had always been quite a bright child, and I soon found myself in the top grammar stream class, which is where I remained throughout my entire secondary education. I was very bright, however, due to my laziness, on completing my education in 1970 I eventually attained two O Levels and not the eight that were predicted.

"I WANT TO BE A COPPER WITH A DOG"

I think it was around Year 4 that the careers week arrived at Monks Park School. I must have been fourteen or fifteen years of age. Because of the school's proximity to the Filton Aerospace (BAC Airplane Works or British Aerospace as I believe they were called), lots of the boys were interested in engineering apprenticeships. This was certainly not for me. I never have in any way been practical. Even today, if a new plug requires putting on a length of electric cable then Linda, my wife, is the person who does the job. What is ironic is that our son, Adam, is a qualified electrician and building project manager and one of our daughters, Laura, has a university degree. It appears that our children inherited my brains but their mother's work ethic – thank goodness they are not as lazy as me!

It soon became apparent to me that any form of hands-on, practical apprenticeship was a definite no-no for me. Just to enhance this fact and confirm that this was the case, a little story. In Year 2 when I was about twelve years old I had the misfortune to have to make two practical items in the woodwork class. It was decided by the teacher that I would make a wooden toothbrush rack and a towel rail. These two bathroom accessories were going to be gifts for my nan. My nan and pop were Percy and Irene Chaplin. They were my dad's parents, and they lived at Lena Street in Easton, Bristol. My dad was an only child, and I was their only grandchild. They adored me, and I loved them to bits.

Over about four months, I somehow managed to create the wooden bathroom accessories and I can recall words like 'mortise and tenon joints' and 'dowelling rods' being mentioned in the construction of these fine pieces of wooden craft. When the final day came and the toothbrush holder and towel rail had been sanded and varnished, I can still recall the teacher's words to the class as he presented me with these unique, bespoke items. His comments were something like, "In all my years' experience in teaching woodwork, I have never come across two pieces of work where the finished articles contain a higher percentage of filler than actual natural wood." Despite these disparaging remarks, my nan loved both pieces, and they remained proudly installed on her bathroom wall (working perfectly) for many years.

Now, back to the careers week. As mentioned, the local aviation industries were heavily represented, plus one of the local garages and engineering firms was very keen to offer young lads hands-on apprenticeships. There were white collar jobs in banks and insurance companies, all branches of the military (Army, Navy and RAF), the fire brigade, and then there was the police (Bristol Constabulary, to be precise).

Bristol had its very own police force. It numbered about one thousand men in total. One very interesting thing that immediately appealed to me was the fact that Bristol Constabulary operated a police cadet unit. This was a very small unit of no more than thirty young boys and girls in total. The average cadetship was about eighteen months, starting at around seventeen and a half years of age, and your cadetship continued until you were nineteen years of age, whereupon you joined the constabulary as a constable.

When it came to the police presentation, Sgt Mike Massey (the recruiting sergeant) really knew his stuff. Their slideshow and brochures were chic and ultra-professional. In hindsight, Sgt Massey was no fool. They did not show you the poor old bobby on the beat, pounding the pavements in the pouring rain trying door handles non-stop. They did not show you the mountains of paperwork that were created every time you arrested a shoplifter. They certainly did not show you the horrible road accidents or sudden death bodies that all bobbies encounter sooner or later.

What they did show you were police officers on large, fast motorbikes, in flashy Jaguar patrol cars, on horseback; police frogmen of the underwater search unit and last but not least the police dog handlers with their police dogs. Wow – that was it; I was sold! I was going to become a police dog handler! Little did I know that I would have to wait about eleven years, until October 1978, to fulfil my dream.

Just prior to me joining the cadets, amazing news hit the Chaplin household. I was now eighteen years old and had long ago given up on the idea of a brother or sister, or even a dog. Then right out of the blue, something happened. Since 1956, my parents had not been practising any form of birth control, due to the fact that after her miscarriage in 1956 my mum was told she could no longer have children. My mum had been feeling unwell, and had put on some weight. Upon going to the doctors, she discovered that she was in fact pregnant (a miracle!) and my sister Penny Jayne was born on 16th January 1971. Mum still said, "We are not having any dogs!" I was about four months into my cadetship.

I joined the Bristol Constabulary Cadet Corps on Monday 1st September 1970 as Police Cadet 21. Before I could join, I had to pass the entrance exam, as I had failed 75% of my O Levels! I sailed through this exam and found myself on the fifth floor of New Bridewell in the Cadet Office with approximately fifteen or sixteen other new cadets, both female and male. On that day, lifelong friendships were formed: Keith Sanders (who became my best man in 1975, and I his three months earlier), Larry Mathieson, Neil Barnes, Alan Ferris, Ian Appleton, Dick Powell, plus the girls, Janet Long, Alison Cooke, Chris Pickett and Glynis from Plymouth. I got on very well with everyone, and to me this police cadetship was brilliant.

Sgt Bob Carpenter and WPC Sally Beard were in control. The boss was Chief Inspector Alan Hayden. We were junior cadets. The older cadets, who were attached to divisions and almost ready to join as constables, had the likes of Peter Moore, Bill Blake and Dianne Hall amongst their ranks. I thrived on the discipline and enjoyed all of the physical and sporting activities that were encouraged. As junior cadets, we had a number of month-long attachments to complete (some residential), which were all aimed at broadening our experiences and giving us a taste of real life in the big, wide world.

I had four notable attachments, each one lasting four weeks. Firstly, I had four weeks at the Dockland Settlement on the corner of City Road and Brigstocke Road in St Pauls (later to be the centre of the St Pauls riots in 1980). This was an inner city youth club ran by a guy called Trevor Wade for the benefit of the local ethnic minority juveniles. Trevor had me painting and decorating, plus other manual tasks that, to be honest, I did not excel at. However, I did learn a lot about life in a deprived area and I certainly met a few faces that I would see time and time again during my future police career.

Next came a four-week stay at Greenhill House in Timsbury in Somerset. This was a residential stay at a Leonard Cheshire charity home, and I fully enjoyed it. I did not go home at weekends, but stayed and worked for nothing. I was helping to look after physically and mentally disabled men and women, which I found extremely humbling and gratifying. I honestly forget the number of soiled bottoms I changed, or puddles of vomit or urine that I cleared up. It was a fantastic experience for a seventeen-year-old city boy. Two things I particularly recall are the cook, a lady called Birdy who made fantastic puddings and cakes but would not tolerate anyone whistling in her kitchen – if you whistled she would explode! The other was the boss of the place, a Major Pears. This old retired army officer took everything for granted, and when I had completed my full four weeks, having also worked three of my four weekends off (during one of which I spent a whole Sunday morning mowing the huge lawns), he gave my report the following endorsement: *Peter Chaplin – a good, sound, average cadet.*

My next attachment was amazing. I was sent to live for four weeks (with no time off) at Tuxwell Farm, Spaxton, Somerset. This livestock and arable farm was owned by Mr Tom Merchant, chairman of the local Conservatives. One of his sons, John, was still at home and helped run the farm. My time here was both very hard and remarkably enjoyable. I started work at 5am when I would bring the herd of cows in for milking, and then I would clean the cowsheds until 8am. It was then breakfast time, after which I would go out in the fields to mend fences and hedges. Lunchtime was 1pm, and then we would clean the barns or cut hedges. It was then time for afternoon milking, followed by a 5pm tea, another two hours helping in and around the farmyard and then at 8pm we would go in, have a wash, and go down to the pub, the Queen Victoria in Spaxton.

John Merchant was my hero. He was a few years older than me, and a true giant of a man. John was the hardest and strongest guy I had ever met. Halfway through my stay my mate and fellow cadet Larry Mathieson came down and stayed the weekend. He agreed that it was a brilliant attachment with marvellous farm-fresh food, plus when I finished Tom Merchant gave me a £5 note (a fortune in 1971) for all of the extras I had done over the month.

My fourth attachment was a dream come true. I had four weeks at the Bristol Constabulary Sports Ground at Kingsweston in Bristol. I was under the command of the head groundsman, Mr John Fotheringham. It was an 8am–4pm day, where duties included marking out the football and rugby pitches, cutting the grass, painting the pavilion and numerous other tasks.

However, the most fantastic news for me was that the sports ground was where the Bristol police dog section did a large amount of its dog training. Sometimes up to three days a week, three or four handlers plus dogs would turn up at Kingsweston to train in such exercises as obedience, distance control, long downs, criminal work, standoffs and open-air quartering (I will explain these terms fully later on). It was at Kingsweston where I first put on the protective leather sleeve and allowed my arm to be subjected to the bone-crunching pressure of a full-on dog bite. Those bites hurt; they pinched the skin and left bruises. Many a time, handlers would shove me up into the branches of one of the trees that wrapped around the sports ground, in order that their dogs could be let loose to locate my scent on the wind in open-air quartering. I loved it in every sense. I was beginning to become known, whilst at the same time coming to recognise various handlers and their dogs.

Those four weeks gave me an up-close-and-personal insight into the section. Handlers such as Derek Gardner, Norman Oliver, Dick Burton, Cyril Haddy, Tom Hornsby, Pete Bush and John Carpenter, not forgetting Terry Connell, were identified in my eyes as heroes and blokes to whom I would aspire to be. I was now more convinced than ever that I wanted to become a dog man, and that my mum's phrase, "We're not having a dog" would one day become irrelevant.

The time I spent working with the guys from the Bristol dog section zoomed by.

LIFE IN THE CADETS

1st September 1970

On that first day the new intake had a brief introduction to cadet life, and we met one or two of the more senior established cadets who outlined what awaited us in the next eighteen months.

I was seventeen and a half, and as mentioned previously I do have the gift of the gab (it's probably the only gift I possess), so within minutes I was nattering away to everybody, boys and girls alike. To use today's parlance, I was 'networking furiously'.

As I said in the beginning, we were only a small unit; about thirty in total. What that meant was that you all had to get on. For example, because I think we only had sixteen male cadets, it meant that everybody was in the rugby team. Most of us were also in the cricket and football teams, too.

The male and female cadets got on very well and there were the inevitable romances starting and stopping occasionally. In fact, some cadets did go on to marry each other. Not me – I finally married a half-Sicilian beauty by the name of Linda. Everyone reckons that she had defective eyesight, otherwise what did she see in me? (Replies on a postcard please to Specsavers, PO Box 999, Doo-Daly Buildings, Soggy Bottom, Berkshire.)

One thing that was brilliant about the cadets was the outward bound camp at the Fedew Farm on the Mynydd Llangattock in the Brecon Beacons. This really was character-building stuff, with rock climbing, caving, orienteering, canoeing and camping. This was for a month, and I believe it was held annually, around November time.

The instructors were all police officers who were ex-army PTIs. When you were a senior cadet (in Year 2) you might be lucky enough to go back over for a month and be one of the camp cooks, which meant that you had more grub and you could have a hot daily shower rather than a cold one.

One quick funny story that I must tell you about our month in the Brecon Beacons was when we were off on one of the four-day hikes over the mountains. We were trained in orienteering and map reading and everyone was split up into three-man tents for the sleeping arrangements every night. I recall that on this trip our patrol consisted of me, Andy Allan (who went on to become an inspector) and a cadet from Norfolk by the name of Mike Fell. I believe that our outward bound courses were quite well received, and a number of other forces used to send cadets on them if there were vacancies.

Every night the directing staff met up with us all at the designated map reference campsite to check that all was well, and amongst other things they gave you the food rations for the following day. Every three-man tent had a small paraffin primus stove and you were expected to cook your own evening meal once you had set camp for the night.

Well, on this particular evening, yours truly, Egon Ronay II, was the master chef preparing the evening meal for Mike, Andy and myself. The menu was tinned corn beef with instant mash and Errin dried peas, all washed down with a delicious mug of hot chocolate made with powdered milk. Now bear in mind, what you had is what you ate, 'cause there wasn't anything else! Anyone can make a mistake, can't they? Unfortunately, I got the powdered spud and the powdered milk mixed up and we had that unique Brecon delicacy of corned beef, peas and chocolate flavoured potatoes!

Don't knock it till you've tried it.

During my time as a cadet we relocated from New Bridewell to Kingsweston House. I must tell you about the occasions when Clarence broke Sgt Carpenter's jaw and the time we met Prince Philip.

Whilst training for the cadet open day, Clarence (Larry Mathieson) vaulted the pommel horse with a little too much enthusiasm and smacked Sgt Bob Carpenter right in the face with his size 13 plimsolls! Poor Sgt Carpenter did not know what hit him. This same experience was enjoyed by many of Larry's opponents on the rugby field on many occasions in the years to come.

It was Larry again who had the privilege of meeting HRH the Duke of Edinburgh at Monks Park School in 1971. The Royal VIP was in Bristol to officiate at a Duke of Edinburgh Award ceremony. As cadets involved in the scheme, we provided a guard of honour at the entrance to the school, and as Larry was the tallest (6'4"), he was the obvious cadet to stop and natter with HRH. Bender Barnes at 5'8" didn't stand a chance.

The other good thing about the cadets was that you were getting an inside view, so to speak, of life in the police service. Playing sport for police teams helped to integrate you. I played for the force football team, and guys like Keith Saunders and Ian Appleton represented the force at both rugby and football, whilst Larry and Alan Ferris were also in the rugby squad.

Sometimes we had to serve at the officers' mess in Old Bridewell. I remember the time my mate Saunders had his thumb in the ACC's soup! There was also the time when Richard Griffiths was on door duty at Old Bridewell on a Saturday morning and said to Chief Constable George Twist (because he did not recognise him), "Oi, mate, shut the door, please."

Great times, great fun and friends that have remained until this day.

Would I do it again? YES, YES, YES!

GOODBYE CADETS, HELLO CHANTMARLE

Constable 115E (in training) Peter Chaplin joined the Bristol Constabulary as a police constable on 4th April 1972. I was sworn in with the Bristol City Council Watch Committee and travelled to the District Police Training Centre at Chantmarle in Dorset. I was in Class 237a from 9th April 1972 to 7th July 1972.

This was it – no messing! Although a small proportion of the recruits were ex-cadets, there were quite a few older ex-services personnel and guys in their mid-twenties from all sorts of jobs in Civvy Street. I loved it from day one! I enjoyed the discipline and the camaraderie. However, I made a fatal mistake in the first month that nearly ended my police career before it had hardly begun.

Do you recall me saying I only got two O Levels when I should have got all of the eight I sat? Well, here I am at training school and I am cruising. We had to learn police powers and definitions parrot-fashion. I did the minimum required. At weekends back in Bristol I would be out with my mates and my girlfriend. Studying was for the 'keeners' and 'do-gooders'. I didn't need to swot on my days off – did I?

I did just about enough in the classroom test and court practicals. I was still cruising and enjoying the lifestyle. Little was I to know that a very hard lesson was about to be learned. After the first four weeks came the first of three examinations. The three-hour exam was on all we had been taught in the first four weeks. There were forty of us in total on Course 237. We were 237a, and our class instructor was an absolute legend by the name of Sgt Bert Barker, of

Bristol Police (Bert went on to become my section sergeant at Trinity Road in 1976). Like us, the other class, 237b, was made up of officers from the following regional police forces: Bristol, Somerset & Bath, Gloucestershire, Wiltshire, Dorset & Bournemouth, Devon, and Cornwall. Upon returning to Chantmarle for the start of week five, the exam results were published and showed the following: in fortieth position and last place with 48% was Constable 115E, Peter Chaplin, Bristol Constabulary.

My feet did not touch the ground. Firstly, I had an interview and a strong reprimand from Superintendent Rees, the Deputy Commandant. He wiped the floor with me, shouting, cursing and telling me how lazy I had been and what a disgrace I was to the Bristol Constabulary, and in particular my class instructor and fellow Bristol officer, namely Sgt Bert Barker. I felt terrible! Worse than I had ever felt in my life. Then I was hauled in to see the Commandant Chief Supt. Reed. Mr Reed truly was an officer and a gentleman. He did not rant and rave – he didn't have to. He simply said he was considering sending me back to my home force as I was 'unlikely to become'. As a new officer you are on a two-year probationary period and during this time your force can dispense with your services. The wide-ranging police expression for this is simple: 'unlikely to become'. I pleaded with Mr Reed for a second chance, an opportunity to mend the errors of my ways. After keeping me waiting for twenty-four hours, he summoned me back into his office and told me this was my last chance to display to the training staff that I was not lazy and I did have what it takes to become a police officer.

MONTH TWO AT CHANTMARLE

It was now time for me to get my head down and get on with it. Weekends were spent at home studying, still living with Mum and Dad and my sister in Lockleaze. I can honestly say that in the second month I did not go out on a weekend – I don't think I even had a beer during that period. One slight interruption to the drudgery of constant studying was the visit from the Dorset & Bournemouth police dog section. This was on our R&R Wednesday afternoon period. Not everyone was into it, but I loved it. I did volunteer to put the sleeve on and be bitten, but my offer was declined.

The thought of a future career on a dog section was still at the back of my mind. However, my immediate plan was to pass exam number two and stay on the course. I could not wait for the exam. I was swotted up to the eyeballs. I really thought, come on, bring it on, I am ready!

The exam was on eight weeks of tuition. The exam was sat, and on the following Monday the result sheet read: *In second place with 84%, Constable 115E Chaplin – Bristol Constabulary.* Brilliant, I thought – I've shown 'em! Now who's the daddy?! Another big mistake.

"Constable 115E Chaplin, Bristol Constabulary, to see the Deputy Commandant Supt. Rees." This was the greeting bellowed at me by my class sergeant, Sgt Bert Barker. I marched into the deputy's office in full uniform; helmet, salute, etc.

Supt. Rees then gave me a dressing-down as severe as the first one. He basically said, "You achieved 84% in exam two, but only

48% in exam one. You really were a lazy shit in the first exam." Talk about pressure!

I continued swotting and learning my powers and definitions parrot-fashion. No rest at all, and no easing up whatsoever. In the final exam (all thirteen weeks' lessons to be tested) I came second with 94.5%, beaten only by Colin Drummond of Gloucestershire who scored 95%. I won the runner-up book prize of Class 237: an Oxford Concise Dictionary, awarded to me by the Deputy Chief Constable of Gloucestershire, Mr D. Smith Esq.

Training school was over and I returned to real police duty in mid-July at A Division Centre, Group 4.

GROUP 4
A DIVISION CENTRAL

My new permanent police number was Constable 150A in the Bristol Constabulary. My mum, incidentally, used to tell everyone that because I had been a cadet I wasn't a police constable; I was in fact a police officer.

After a week's leave I reported for duty at the Central Police Station in Nelson Street, Bristol. I joined Group 4 at A Division Central. There were about twenty-five constables on a group, three sergeants and one inspector. My boss was an absolute legend. His name was Inspector Bernie Phelan. He was a bachelor in his early sixties and he did not have long until retirement.

The two established sergeants were legends also. Firstly, there was Mike 'Slim' Hawkins. His nickname came from the fact that he was an ex-Bristol rugby player and he must have had a sixty-inch chest. He was only about 5' 8" tall, but his physique was immense; he was no 7A. The other sergeant was an amazing guy called John Broadbelt, or JB, as he was affectionately known. JB was a larger-than-life character. He had nicknames for everyone, and at the time the TV programme *The Two Ronnies* was very popular. On my group there was a big, young tough guy from Nottingham called Andy Woodward. Well, in JB's eyes I became Charley Farley and Andy became Piggy Malone. (Tragically, Andy Woodward died in an off-duty motorcycle accident about two years later.) JB was 21A. Also in our group was an acting sergeant called Keith Savoury. Keith was a smashing bloke; he had passed his sergeant and inspector exams and was performing duties as an acting sergeant prior to getting promoted.

I was the new nineteen-year-old, skinny, red-faced sprog, straight out of training school and the brunt of everyone's practical jokes. This happened to all new recruits, but being an ex-gadget (cadet), it was worse. Normally, you would long for a few months to go by in order that a brand new bobby, straight from Chantmarle, would join the group and he could become the new focus of attention, relieving the pressure on you. In practice, what happens is that the next new bobby is a ten-year ex-army veteran, who in the life experience stakes leaves you at the bottom of the pile. However, my ability to get on with folk helped enormously, and I knew a few faces in the nick. I had been a reasonable footballer and I had been playing for both the full Bristol police team and the A division football side for about eighteen months.

One of the inspectors at Central was a huge, hairy man called Bob Bates (centre half). It seemed funny saluting him and calling him 'Sir' at work, but then on the football pitch on Saturday or Wednesday afternoon calling him Bob.

When you turn up as a brand new probationary constable fresh out of the box, you are allocated for one month to a poor sod called a tutor constable. I say poor sod because for one month this officer works his socks off, trying to introduce you to as many varied offences and situations as possible. The group as a whole love having a new proby on the group because it means that every shit job, boring assignment, awkward sudden death or shitty juvenile shoplifter in that month will be directed the proby's way. You can't argue with it; it's the way that it has always been done and it's the way to gain vital knowledge and experience.

In my case, my tutor was a tall, slim officer called David Forward. Now Dave was a lovely guy, but his future lay in communications and to be honest Dave was more of a radio geek. With the greatest respect, he was not a Rambo, Action Man type of officer.

I remember the chaos I caused early one Monday morning when we had been allocated the traffic point on College Green adjacent to the statue of Queen Victoria and opposite the Royal Hotel. You had to be on point by certain time, as a guy by the name of Curly

Grant, the Chief Superintendent of the Traffic Division, came into work every morning via this route. The only traffic control duty we had done was a ten-minute session at Chantmarle and a short stint on our local procedure course at the junction of Shirehampton Road and Long Cross, in Lawrence Weston. It was very quiet traffic-wise and the time we did this, we had to wait for a car to come along in order for us to stop it.

So Dave went on point first and I duly watched for ten minutes as he waved and directed traffic to go or stop as he saw fit. With a lull in the flow of cars he came off point and said, "Over to you, Pete."

I had my long white traffic coat on and was wearing my pristine white gloves; if nothing else at least I looked the part. This was one of the busiest and most congested points in the city and I could not find a suitable gap to get out into the centre of the road. I looked at Dave for advice and he said, "You are a constable who has the authority to stop motor vehicles." He had hardly finished when I confidently strode out into the road with my hand held up with the No. 1 stop signal, and *BANG – BANG – BANG – BANG – BANG*: a five-car shunt courtesy of 150A. We then spent the next thirty minutes with motorists exchanging names and addresses and insurance details. I wonder if Curly Grant noticed anything untoward that morning?

Despite this we got through the month and by about the end of August 1972, I was out solo on the beat!

GOING SOLO

Well, this was it! Late turn (2pm–10pm) at Central, and I think it was a Thursday. You always got to work about thirty minutes before your shift because you had to parade for duty a quarter of an hour prior to the shift starting. This meant in this case that the early turn (6am–2pm) were covering up until 2pm. Then at 2pm sharp, we were briefed and ready to go.

At Central, Alpha 1 was always the early car. It came on at 1.30pm–9.30pm for a late turn, to cover any incidents and hopefully prevent the early turn getting lumbered. The two other Panda cars (Morris 1000s with a huge police sign on the roof) were Alpha 3 working from Central and Alpha 2 working out of a small satellite station (River Station) in The Grove, down in the city docks area.

The River Station, with its Skipper, Sgt Hughie Sennington (an old, mature footballer who played into his fifties), was in my mind the 'gem station' of the Bristol police. There were no senior officers around, only one skipper and five PCs, plus they had two police launches to swan around the docks in, and the larger launch was capable of cruising down the River Avon when the tide and circumstances allowed.

I did perform the occasional shift at the River Station with Brian Maggs and Eric Selly. It was a favourite tea stop for traffic and the police motorcyclists.

BACK TO MY FIRST DAY SOLO

I was in the parade room at about 1.35pm in full uniform with my helmet, pocket book and truncheon ready to 'produce my appointments'. This is when you stand to attention and produce your pocket notebook, truncheon and torch for the inspector to view and confirm that you are compliant. Believe it or not, we also had to pull our trousers up from the ankles to demonstrate that we were wearing the regulation black or navy blue socks.

Normally, before the parade starts you would look at all of the relevant up-to-date files and photographs from your divisional collator. These would have all the information about the latest crime trends, wanted criminals, etc. The duty inspector would then walk in. We would all stand to attention and he would take the parade. The senior sergeant would have the duty board and the entire subdivision was divided into about twenty-five beats (area of patrol).

On this, my first solo day, I was allocated 'Broadmead on the first'. The Broadmead shopping centre was divided between the first and third beat areas of the subdivision. This meant I had the Castle Park side of Broadmead. This covered Fairfax House, Woolworths, and the large supermarket on Broad Weir. Basically, if you got Broadmead on the first or third, more often than not you ended up with a prisoner for shoplifting. Inspector Phelan read out a list of recent stolen vehicles and wanted persons. By about 2.05pm I was stood in the Central Station office waiting to be issued with my light blue two-piece (receiver and transformer) Pye personal radio. These had serial numbers on them and it was drummed into us how expensive they were, and how we weren't to lose them under any circumstances.

By 2.10pm I was out on patrol in Broadmead and by 2.15pm I had directed my first Welsh visitor in the general direction of Bristol Zoo. In those early days probationers were expected to submit at least one piece of process per shift. This meant at least one traffic offence form had to be submitted to JB or Slim Hawkins at the end of every tour of duty. In addition to this, we had IR (incident report) forms. These went from IR 1 to IR 9, and the two favourites to get your name and number on paper for were the IRs for defective paving-slab trip hazards and the one for night duty (the unusual light?). This was where a shop had had its lights left on and it was unusual for it to be so. (I think senior officers thought safe-breakers were at work.) I believe an officer on duty the following day would call on the particular premises to confirm that all was in order. With regards to traffic offences on 'Broadmead on the first', the favourite place to nab a motorist was at the junction of the far end of Fairfax Street with Broad Weir. At this junction, the City Council decided to make it a no right turn. This meant that to get to Bristol Bridge you had to turn left and drive up to the *Evening Post* roundabout in order to travel back up to Broad Weir and the top of Union Street.

On this afternoon, I was too naive to hide in the shadows like a big game hunter or undercover SAS operative waiting to strike. Like a plonker, I stood right on the junction and as Cilla would say, "Surprise, surprise!" Every motorist complied precisely and everyone turned left as the local bylaw demanded.

Then to my horror at about 3.15pm, the radio operator (Sgt Den Letty) gave out a gut-wrenching call: "Alpha control, Alpha control to 150." No reply. Again, "Alpha control, Alpha control to 150."

Shit! I thought. That's me. "Go ahead, over!" I said, and Den Letty bellowed at me, "Answer your radio first time! Now make your way to the fruit and veg shop in Broad Weir – there is a problem."

The problem was that the shop's fruit and veg display had encroached too far out onto the pavement, and pedestrians were being impeded. My first reportable offence, single crew. The shop owner was reported for obstruction of the footway and prosecuted. *Dixon of Dock Green* and *Z Cars* – eat your heart out! Pete Chaplin, 150A, ace crime fighter is now in town. Criminals beware – Bristol's answer to Dirty Harry has arrived! Do you feel lucky, punk?

FUNNY STORIES AT CENTRAL

During my first three years at Central many incidents occurred, some exciting and some funny. I thought I'd share a few with you.

Sticky Fingers and Sticky Ears

One thing you learn very quickly as a new copper is to look after your gloves and torch (because they will go missing). On one of my early night shifts I was distracted and inadvertently left my black leather gloves on the station office desk. In the early 1970s the age of the computer had not yet arrived and lots of messages were handwritten and then stuck into the Station Occurrence book with Gloy glue.

When I returned to collect my gloves I walked outside the nick, and as I slid my hands into my gloves I came into contact with about ten fluid ounces of Gloy in each glove. Nice!

The other occasion Gloy and I met was on another night shift and I was allocated the 'goldfish bowl' at the front of the main station office. On nights it was customary to have a probationer situated there from 10pm till midnight, to take a lot of the mundane enquires away from the station office staff. This small glass cubicle was the first point of call for members of the public who were attending Central in order to comply with an HORT 1 (Home Office Road Traffic) that they had been issued whilst driving, as it requested them to produce their driving documents at a police station within a prescribed number of days.

Now the telephone line in the goldfish bowl was an extension of the station office's, so when the station office phone rang the goldfish bowl phone rang simultaneously.

On this particular night I had only just come on duty and sat in the goldfish bowl when the station office phone rang. A voice from the station office bellowed, "Pick that up, Charley."

I duly obliged and a voice on the phone simply said, " Have you got a sticky ear, mate?"

And yes, I did: the ear piece was covered in Gloy. Happy days.

First Prisoner

It is nearly unbelievable but my first ever prisoner (shoplifting a leather jacket from Debenhams in Broadmead) went not guilty and elected trial at the Crown Court in Bristol. Going to Crown Court with your first arrest is unusual! The accused was a young man from a well-known criminal family from South Bristol. He had been stopped about a yard from the ground-floor exit, which at the time was within the food hall of Debenhams in Bristol. His defence was that he was still within the store and he was wearing the leather jacket to see what it looked like in daylight.

His defence barrister was an old hand, and was a formidable adversary to such a young and inexperienced cop as myself. When I was in the witness box giving evidence he said to me in a mock-derisory manner, "Constable Chaplin, you are obviously a man of the world, an officer of immense experience, an officer who has dealt with lots of crimes and criminals in your time. In your experience, is it not the case that store detectives normally allow their alleged suspect to leave their premises to in fact *prove* some level of intent to steal, because in this case my client was still within the confines of Debenhams."

The jury were tittering and giggling, the prosecution barrister was smirking – even the judge was smiling. Here I was, my first arrest, nineteen years old, skinny and spotty – basically a nerd in uniform. I don't think I was even shaving at the time.

I replied in a very shaky voice, "Sir, this is my first arrest as a police officer, and in my experience the store detectives always stop their suspects before they leave their store and have the opportunity to run away."

The judge said, "Thank you, officer," and the villain was duly convicted. He was only in his early twenties and already had five or six convictions for theft!

The Day He Was De-Loused
Central in 1972, Late Autumn, 2pm Late Turn

Whilst on parade, the parade sergeant gave out details of a vagrant character, very well known on A Division. He was a Jamaican who would sit and play a banjo, busking in the Broadmead area, but he was wanted for fine default, and a warrant was in existence for his arrest.

I was still very new and had not had many arrests. As I walked into Broadmead I suddenly saw this man busking and playing his banjo outside of Woolworths. In ten seconds he was under arrest. Within two minutes he was in Alpha 1 on route to Central.

He was in the initial stages of being booked in when JB (Charge Sgt John Broadbelt) yelled at me, "Charley, you f*****g idiot – what have you done?!" He went berserk at me, cussing and swearing, and suddenly the charge room emptied. As he was leaving, JB yelled at me, "Charley – look at his head!" It was then I noticed that the vagrant's entire scalp was alive and moving. He had fleas, mites, ticks – you name it, he had it. I had to drive him down to the City Council's de-lousing unit in Cattle Market Road, where we were both stripped naked and bathed in disinfectant. All my uniform was burnt and Alpha 1 and the charge office had to be fumigated. I was not the most popular bunny on the block for quite a while!

Buckets of Water and Capes Don't Mix

Nights again (the most interesting events happened on nights). I was patrolling Trenchard Street by the Entertainment Centre and Hatchett pub. It was a cold winter's night at about 1am. As I walked under the bridge with Park Street above me, near to the Mauritania pub I could see that someone had thrown a road lamp, full of paraffin with a naked flame, up onto the windowsill of a small restaurant in Trenchard Street. This windowsill was a good ten feet high. I ran into the restaurant and to save calling the fire brigade I asked for a bucket of water and a bar stool to stand on. The lamp was burning, but thankfully it had not set the wooden window frame alight. I gingerly stood on the stool as one of the restaurant staff handed me up a bucket full to the brim with water. I was on an uneven pavement, wearing my cape, and as I balanced and tried to extricate my arms from under my cape to be in a position to throw the water, I got everything wrong! Whilst trying to throw the water at the burning lamp (which was still a good two feet above me), I lost my grip on the bucket, my footing and my balance, and the water ended up going all over me. The bucket was on my head and I fell off of the stool! By now, someone had called the fire brigade and within ten seconds of them arriving, a small, thin water hose had doused the burning lamp. I was left as a soggy mess on the floor!

Curry and Cape

Being allocated Stokes Croft as a foot patrol on nights, especially in winter, was like winning the lottery. This was due to two main reasons:

1. You could always get your free curry and chips from the Chinese chippy in Jamaica Street. Winter was a bonus because you could hide your tray under your cape. Slowly walking up The Croft and then Cheltenham Road with that lovely hot tray of goodness under your cape, you could snaffle a curry-laden chip with your little wooden fork – pure heaven!
2. There was the bakery in Cheltenham Lane, just up past Colston's Girls' School. From about 4am you could nab a cup of coffee and a freshly cooked jam doughnut, which was marvellous.

Now one night just after midnight I was at Station Road, Montpelier. It was a bitterly cold winter's night. I was wearing my cape, and I still had a good half a tray of curry and chips in my right hand under my cape. My left hand was holding my little wooden fork, and I was just contemplating the next mouthful when, oh dear, around the corner comes the inspector's car with Inspector Bernie Phelan driving and JB (Sgt John Broadbelt) in the front passenger seat. They knew exactly what I was up to!

As they pulled up, JB said, "Charley Farley – don't you normally salute the inspector?" I hurriedly had to swap hands under my cape, moving the tray of chips from right to left so that I could salute. These occasions were termed street visits, and you had to produce your pocket book for the sergeant to sign. All the while the smell of curry and chips was seeping through my cape's buttonholes. They kept me chatting for ages, talking about bullshit, basically – crime trends, unusual lights; suspicious vehicles in the area. Then they drove off slowly, to my relief.

Suddenly they stopped and the car slowly reversed until JB's window was level with me. He opened the window about three inches and said, sarcastically, "Inspector Phelan said don't let your chips get cold!" They then quietly drove off down Cheltenham Road.

TRANSFER TO TRINITY ROAD

In early 1975, I was fortunate enough to transfer from Group 4 Central to Group 4 Trinity Road. There were many reasons for wanting to transfer from the A Division HQ to the smaller Trinity Road subdivision. Some of the reasons are as follows:

1. The top boss at Trinity in 1975 was a chief inspector. Unlike Central, which was adjacent to the Force Head Quarters, there was no possibility of bumping into senior officers and ACPO rank bosses.
2. The group was about a quarter the size of Central's – one inspector, one sergeant and eight or nine constables.
3. Everyday life in general was a lot less regimental, and the relationship between the chief inspector and the constables seemed far more relaxed.
4. You sat down on parade with a cup of tea.
5. Parking of your private cars was a lot easier and more convenient. At Central you quite often had to park in Kingsdown and then walk a mile to work. Consequently, it was a long walk back to your car at the end of the shift.
6. The guys at Trinity were, on the whole, a little more experienced and consequently they seemed a little more competent, and perhaps were cut a little more slack.
7. We had three area cars and a spare car, and although you performed foot patrol quite often you did seem to ride more in police cars than you did at Central.

The general police duties were a lot more varied at Trinity. There was the tinderbox of St Pauls that always had the capability to explode, and five years later in 1980 it did explode, and the inner city St Pauls riots occurred.

Also, there were all the other issues associated with the inner city, where the ethnic minorities were housed. We had residential areas like Easton, The Dings, Montpellier, Eastville and so on, with all their associated problems. Two things we didn't get so much of were shoplifters and Section 5 public order offences.

I remained at Trinity for just over a year, and in early 1976 I was seconded to the special services square for eighteen months. However, I cannot leave the subject of my Trinity Road experiences without sharing the following account with you. This is probably one of the most amazing incidents that I ever attended in my twenty-eight-year police service.

I have been the first officer at the scene in two murders in my career. This first one in 1976 was horrendous. The second, in 1996 (7th January), was when I arrested a youth for murder – in my front room. As amazing as this may seem, it is true!

A Sudden Death to Remember

I can recall it like it was yesterday. It was a Friday early turn and I was double-crewed with a good friend of mine (I will call him John for the purpose of this tale). We were crewing the St Pauls car known as Alpha 4. A Friday early turn meant that we were just about to start our long weekend

We had already had grub at 9am and we were parked up in Montpellier when the radio burst into life: "Alpha 4, make your way to a sudden death at such-and-such an address at the top end of Montpellier, near to the Fairfield Grammar School." Details of the deceased were then given to us.

I was driving and John said to me, "Pete, do me a favour – drop me back at Trinity. I've got some paperwork to complete before the weekend, and I am off to Devon surfing this afternoon." It transpired that John was off on a jolly to Croyde and didn't want to run the risk of missing his lift at 2pm. He continued to plead, "Come on, it's only sudden death. It doesn't need two of us." So like a good buddy, I dropped him off at the nick and then made my way to the address I had been given over the radio.

These were large Victorian houses, and as I pulled up an elderly chap appeared from a house opposite and told me that the lady had had a brain haemorrhage and was in the front upstairs bedroom. I quickly learned from this old chap that the deceased lady was well into her eighties, and that she had a middle-aged lodger who used to leave the front door unlocked to enable him to gain access to the premises to check on her every morning. I went into the house via the unsecured front door and made my way up to the bedroom.

What confronted me when I opened the door was horrendous! As I took those first few steps into the room I heard *meow...scratch*. Three or four cats came charging out of the room. There was blood everywhere and tiny bloody paw prints were all over the place. These paw prints were soon on the landing and all down the stairs. Upon looking to my right I saw a large old-fashioned double bed with a metal bedstead. The bedding was covered in blood. There was a figure (albeit slight) under the covers of the bed. The top sheet had been pulled up over the head of the body that was under the bedclothes. I was shaking somewhat, and with every bit of courage I could summon I slowly pulled the bed sheet down about twelve inches, which exposed the head and face of a very elderly lady. This unfortunate soul had suffered horrendous head injuries.

I was thinking to myself, I have no experience of a brain haemorrhage but surely they don't look like this. To me it looks like she had been violently struck with something heavy. Initially, I pulled the cover back over her face and requested immediate assistance over the radio, as I believed that I had a very suspicious death on my hands. I only had four years' service and I was reluctant to use the word 'murder' over the air. I did not want to be ridiculed if I had got it wrong.

This situation changed considerably in the following couple of minutes. My scene of crime training kicked in and I decided that

I should be checking the body for any further injuries. I pulled the sheet down as before, then further down, exposing the lady's neck and shoulders. On pulling down the sheet I discovered that she had also sustained massive injuries to her throat. This prompted a hurried second radio call in which I said, "I want Senior CID ASAP, as I think we have a murder on our hands."

Upon examining further, I discovered that this unfortunate individual had also sustained a stab wound to the chest. My mind was in turmoil, and was racing. Who could have done such a wicked thing? I then started to think about my actions. Have I done everything correctly? What have I cocked up? I decided to quickly have a look around the rest of the house. What if I find another body? The murderer, perhaps? What if the perpetrator has committed suicide downstairs?

Wow – I am glad I did that search! No bodies, no suicides; however, in the first-floor bathroom I found in the washbasin a large carving knife covered in blood (this was later confirmed to be one of the murder weapons).

Now in the distance I could hear two-tone horns, and in about five or six minutes I was joined by the Superintendent in charge at Trinity Road and a host of other officers including the DI and DCI from A Division CID, and eventually the head of Avon & Somerset CID, a Detective Chief Superintendent. Soon there were coppers everywhere. I was instructed to perform various tasks by senior officers; however, in the end I took up position at the front of the house, and for continuity purposes I kept the original running log of the incident from start to finish.

Having never been involved in a major crime before, I was intrigued and engrossed in the detective analysis and procedures. Once again, for continuity I seemed to be involved in all aspects of the quickly moving investigation. I was sitting in on briefings (meetings with senior CID officers). I was eventually being called Peter by the head of the Avon & Somerset Constabulary CID. Another as yet unseen dimension to the crime was soon to be discovered at the post mortem in Backfields. When it came to the post mortem

I soon realised that I had to be in attendance for the continuity of the case. Now, I had been to PMs before, but never from the beginning. Never when every single procedure is carried out.

There was one point during the post mortem when the pathologist expressed his concern that despite the terrible head wound, throat and stab injuries, there was in fact a fourth contributing factor to the individual's death.

"Almonds," he declared, "I can smell almonds." He went on to express his opinion that this lady had been poisoned with cyanide. Laboratory tests later revealed that this was true, and had occurred prior to the other injuries.

A suspect was quickly identified as the old lady's long-standing lodger. This lodger was a middle-aged scientist who worked as an analyst at a large organisation in the West Country. He had no previous convictions whatsoever. He was arrested sometime later when he was found in the Warwickshire area. His motorcar had been observed travelling repeatedly between two junctions on the motorway. This was in the local vicinity of the family home in Warwickshire.

A guilty plea soon followed and the following transpired: Mr Lodger had lodged with the deceased lady for over fifteen years, and for all of that time the old lady had nagged and nagged at him, to the extent that apparently it made his life a misery. She would not relent in her constant moaning. Things must have become so bad that he decided to do away with her by poisoning her with cyanide that he stole from the laboratory where he worked. He was in the habit of making the old lady an early morning beverage (hot chocolate, I believe), and would take it up to her room every morning before he left for work. It would appear that on that fateful morning he took her up the hot chocolate, laced with cyanide. She started to drink it, then became very distressed and started coughing and spluttering. He thought that she was suffering, so he ran downstairs and took the carving knife and cut her throat and stabbed her. In the final act of putting her out of her suffering he administered the blow to the head with a lump hammer. He then covered her over with the bed sheet and left for Warwickshire, where he was later arrested. It was some while later that Mr Neighbourhood Watch made his daily morning call and found her with the 'brain haemorrhage'.

I finally got home on Sunday afternoon, after a very eventful forty-eight hours. Back at the nick on the first night shift, the following Tuesday, all of the talk was about the murder and what a jammy so-and-so John had been for clearing off to Croyde and avoiding all of the commotion.

FUNNY STORIES AT TRINITY

Now that I knew I was going to be going on to the section, the time passed very slowly. I was lucky in that I had a good bunch of guys on my group at Trinity. When I say Trinity, I actually mean the old Avon Vale Junior School in Avon Vale Road, Barton Hill, Bristol. The new Trinity Road Police Station was under construction and for about eighteen months the police subdivision that was Trinity Road was working out of the old school. Coincidentally this was part of my junior school complex that I had attended in 1959–1964.

As mentioned, I had a good group of officers that I worked with at Avon Vale: Colston Chappell, Barry Forsyth and Ted Osteran, to name but a few. As with all nicks, funny incidents occurred along with serious ones, and I thought it would be a good opportunity to lighten the mood somewhat and relate a few funny stories to you all.

Inspector Govier's Near Miss

The boss of the group was Inspector Eric Govier. Eric was a bachelor who lived in Fishponds, Bristol. This was in early 1978. Eric's pride and joy was his Ford Cortina 1600E. To those of you who are not aware, the Cortina 1600E was an iconic motorcar of its day. The inspector had the privilege of having a parking space in the police yard. Now, I must explain that the car park yard at Avon Vale had a distinctive slope to it.

On this particular late turn I was driving Alpha 5. I had come in for grub at 5pm and reversed up against the fence, directly behind Inspector Govier's personal car. Alpha 5 was facing down the slope and was about fifteen yards away from the inspector's 1600E. I then went into the nick for my refreshments.

After about ten minutes, Sgt Bert Barker came hurriedly into the canteen shouting, "1488, you don't know how lucky you are – out into the car park, now!"

In the car park I found Inspector Govier with a very stern expression on his face as he examined every inch of his 1600E.

I had not set the handbrake correctly on Alpha 5, or had left it in gear. To my horror Alpha 5 was not where I had left it. It was now embedded into the wall alongside the inspector's car. The only thing that saved my bacon was that the steering lock was on and when the handbrake clicked off and Alpha 5 rolled forward, it did so at a slight arc, consequently missing Mr Govier's motor by about two inches. If the front wheels had been positioned straight, then Alpha 5 would have ploughed straight into Mr Govier's car. Both Mr Govier and Bert Barker commented on the fact that it was just as well for me that this incident had occurred after their glowing references had already been submitted for my move to dogs. The end result was a bollocking from Supt. Arkell, the subdivision commander.

Practical Jokes on New Probationers
The Nuclear Fallout Scam

We had a new guy on who group who had been in the military for a little while and was a bit of a know-it-all. This was the trick we played on him. A Mufax message (Mufax is an early type of Telex system) was concocted to this effect:

From the British Nuclear Power Authority at Berkeley Nuclear Power Station in Gloucestershire:
There is a remote possibility that a very small amount of radioactive material has seeped out of the power station and possibly made its way into the regional water courses. Scientists at Berkeley have requested that all local police

forces assist in obtaining samples of river water, that once obtained, will be collected and returned to Berkeley for analysis.

For Avon & Somerset Police the task was quite specific. At precisely 4.03am on that day's date (5th June 1978), an officer was asked to attend at Wellington Road, St Jude's, Bristol to obtain a sample of river water (at least three quarters of a pint) from exactly seven inches below the water surface, in midstream. The time of 4am was chosen as it was the unofficial time for tea at Trinity & Central, and was normally the quietest period of the night shift. Prior to the ex-military officer being brought to the scene, every spare A Division copper was hiding in and around the Wellington Road river for a good view.

At about 3.50am Alpha 4 arrived with this officer. Another two officers were already in situ with a wooden ladder (no idea where this came from). The officer had a glass milk bottle with a length of string secured around its neck, and he also carried the Trinity Road station office's twelve-inch wooden ruler. He was instructed to take off his boots and socks, and to roll his trousers up over his knees. The ladder had been placed over the wall that bounded the shallow River Frome that flowed from Frenchay into the city centre. He was helped down the ladder into the cold, fast-flowing current (it was only about eighteen inches deep at that point). He was handed the milk bottle, ruler and a rubber torch. It was now almost 4am, and he only had three minutes to position himself midstream, ready to collect the sample.

Bobbies were appearing from everywhere, trying to get a good view of this truly scientific genius at work. The poor old officer needed three hands to hold the milk bottle, ruler and torch. The inevitable happened and he dropped the torch into the water. Nevertheless, he persevered and at bang on 4.03am he held the neck of the milk bottle seven inches under the surface of the water and collected the sample midstream, and then *flash!* He thought it was lightning, but one of the guys had brought a camera and his efforts were preserved for history! He did finally see the funny side when months later an equally silly prank was played on the latest newcomer.

Ticking Manhole Covers

This next prank was short and simple.

We had had the IRA bomb in Park Street, and the possible threat of IRA activity was real. The task set before the new recruit, recently returned from training school, was to put on a white traffic coat (long white coats that were worn when performing point duty; traffic control, in other words), and whilst one of the Panda cars stopped in the centre of the road with the blue light flashing, the intrepid young officer was to kneel on the road, bend down and put his ear to the manhole cover and listen for the sound of ticking.

I don't know what the isolated early morning motorist must have thought at 4.45am in Midland Road or Ashley Hill when confronted with this officer dressed all in white on his knees listening to manholes!

Shortest Funny Story
Late 1975

On our shift at Trinity Road were me and a really good guy called Colston Chapell. (Colston was also an ex-cadet about two years younger than me.) So you had a Chaplin and a Chapell based on the same group.

There were a few of us in the station office at Avon Vale School. This was the temporary home of Trinity Road nick whilst the new station was being built.

Anyway, we are in the nick and the station office phone rings. Colston picks it up and says, "Colston Chappell."

The person at the other end said, "Oh, I am terribly sorry, I wanted Trinity Road Police," and put the phone down.

Honest, it happened.

More Funny Trinity Tales

Here are four true little stories that occurred in and around 1976, during my first stint at Trinity Road.

I should begin by explaining that Trinity Road nick was truly amazing. It had not changed much since it was built: high ceilings in all the offices and a boiler room that was used for coal.

The first two stories concern our station officer and senior copper by the name of Len Woods. Len was a straight-faced, frizzy-haired, brilliant practical joker.

First Story: He Was in a Hell of a State!

As with most police station stories, these things usually happen at night (no bosses about), and things quieten down after about 4am.

Len was the station reserve office man on Group 4 at Trinity Road. One of his many tasks, especially on nights, was to keep the coal-fired boiler topped up with coal so that it didn't go out. To this end, a pair of large wellington boots were positioned just inside the boiler room; this saved the station reserve getting his shoes filthy, and also kept black, sooty footprints from being trampled all over the nick.

I have already mentioned the high ceilings (possibly twelve to fifteen feet high). To help with the very high windows there were also two very long wooden window openers (these were wooden poles about ten feet long with hooks on the end).

Midway through the night Len had stoked up the boiler and had then brought the soot-laden wellies into the station office. He then, with the use of the long-handled window poles, put the boots on the poles and proceeded to walk across the ceiling.

Well, the result was hilarious! All that was left now was for Len to wait for a member of the public to call in at the nick.

Despite it being the middle of the night, you would still get people coming to report minor crimes or produce driving documents or make complaints about something or someone, or the milkman or early morning cleaners would call in.

Len would engage them in some trivial conversation and then draw their attention to the ceiling. As their eyes focused on the black boot prints across the ceiling they looked on in shock and bemusement.

Len would say, "That fella was so highly strung and upset. He just found out that his wife had run off with his best friend. Poor bugger! We had to peel him off of the ceiling!"

Second Story: Bee on the Window

The next silly little prank that Len used to play was to use a black or blue felt pen to write the letter B on the station office window.

He would wait for a suitable visitor to come into the station office; normally it would be someone producing their driving documents. He would lure them over to the window on the pretext of being in better light to examine their documents. He would position them approximately to the right spot and then shout, "Watch out, there's a bee on the window!" It was priceless!

Third Story: Heavy Showers Forecast

Just for a change, this little story actually occurred not at night but on a hot summer's afternoon in July/August 1976.

The vehicular access in and out of Trinity Road was via a gateway which led directly out onto Trinity Road. This is quite a tricky exit and you always had to stop to check that the road was clear before pulling out.

The kitchen window was on the first floor directly above where Panda cars would have to stop and check for traffic flow.

I can't recall exactly who I had in the car on this hot, sunny afternoon, but I think it was a store detective from Iceland in Easton Road; they had come to the nick to either look at some mug shots of local villains or to make a statement, something of that order. Anyway, I was driving and the store detective was sat behind me in the rear of the Panda car (it was only a two-door Ford Escort, I believe). I think my co-pilot that day was a great character, PC John O'Conner, alias Little Jim.

It was very hot, and I had my driver's side window wound right down, and probably my elbow resting on the open window. I stopped to check for a suitable gap in the traffic coming from my left, when suddenly *whoosh!* Len Woods very kindly poured a bucket of water out of the kitchen window down into the open window of my Panda car. I took eighty per cent of the deluge, the store detective took ten per cent and nearly shit herself, and Little Jim took ten per cent and said, "Sudden downpours were expected today."

It could only happen at Trinity Road!

Fourth Story: the Hangman's Noose

Trinity Road was an old nick. The car entrance was always open; this led into the yard where the Panda cars were parked. Leading off the yard were a number of doors into the station. Also in the yard was a wooden staircase that led into the first-floor recreation room. In those days, doors weren't locked; it was as simple as that.

This is in the spring of 1976. For quite a few sets of nights we had been having a slight problem with one of our local tramps, a vagrant by the name of Roberts, who normally frequented the little park just opposite Trinity Walk, about a hundred yards from the nick.

Roberts had been found in the station a couple of times. During the cold weather he had been found in the vicinity of the boiler room, understandably. However, on this night, Roberts had committed probably one of the top cardinal sins.

The night shift was 10pm until 6am. Refreshments were at 1am or 2am. On this particular night the guys on early grub (1am) had been engaged on a job, therefore it meant all of us were in at 2am. Four of us intended to play a doubles game of snooker in the rec room. Within the force and in the A Division in particular we had a couple of very good snooker players: Chief Inspector Morris Marks and DS Bert Townsend spring to mind. Anyway, in the 70s snooker was very popular.

As we entered the rec room on the first floor we were appalled by the sight that greeted us. Our local vagrant Mr Roberts was laid upon his back on our snooker table, fast asleep! A quick convene and very quiet kangaroo court was arranged. Someone very useful with a length of rope made a passable noose. This said noose was strung up over one of the metal roof struts above the snooker table and was now dangling about a foot above Roberts' head and about two foot in front of him.

Roberts was woken from his slumber by one of the lads shouting in his ear, "Roberts, wake up!" No one wanted to touch him, as he was not the cleanest of individuals. As he suddenly awoke, he saw the noose and screamed out loud.

One of the other guys shouted, "It's the rope for you, Roberts, if you're ever caught in here again!"

With that Roberts was off the table like a shot; he dashed out of the door down the stairs and was never seen on the subdivision again!

SPECIAL SERVICES SQUAD
SECONDED TO SSS FOR 18 MONTHS
FROM UNIFORM DUTIES AT TRINITY ROAD

April 1976–October 1977

This was a brilliant time spent as an undercover covert squad. There were lots of stories, some funny and some very serious. We were basically a squad of one detective inspector, two detective sergeants and twenty detective constables. Primarily, these were thief-catchers. Normally, the special services were considered to be a precursor to joining the CID. To be honest, I could write a book on my special service experiences alone.

There were some great times on special services with a great team of guys, but even greater times were awaiting me on the dog section.

Back to Trinity for a Year

I returned to duty at Trinity Road (with my first haircut in two years) in October 1977. I spent a further year at Trinity (Avonvale) until joining the dogs in 1978. During my time on special services and whilst on my second stint at Trinity the new Trinity Road Police Station was being built.

I finally said goodbye to A Division and Trinity Road on the 21st of October 1978.

Trinity Road Leaving Do

On Saturday 21st October 1978, I had my leaving do at the Central club in Bridewell Police Station. A good turnout of Central & Trinity lads attended.

It had been taken me almost six and a half years after joining as a PC to achieve my goal of getting onto the dog section.

My colleagues kindly gave me a pewter tankard inscribed with one word – "SILENCE" – as a leaving gift.

Anyone would think that I talked a lot!

DOG SECTION INTERVIEW

This is a short introduction to the Avon & Somerset Police Dog Section. This was now around July 1978. Bristol Constabulary had amalgamated with both the Somerset & Bath Constabulary and the Southern Division (South Gloucestershire) of the Gloucestershire Constabulary in April 1974. We were now a force of around 3,200 officers, with forty officers being dog handlers.

The boss was Chief Inspector Dick Cheetham, and the HQ was at Bower Ashton on the outskirts of Bristol. Bower Ashton was the HQ for horses and dogs, and Chief Inspector Cheetham was the horse master. His deputy and boss of the dog section was Inspector Brian Langley. There were then five sergeants; four were based in Bristol, and with their team of four Bristol handlers, they covered the city. As far as I can recall the Staple Hill, Bath and Weston-super-Mare handlers were under the Bristol sergeants' supervision. The remaining officers in the county of Somerset (Taunton, Yeovil and Frome) came under the fifth sergeant, who was based in Taunton. Vacancies were few and far between on the dog section. Normally vacancies only arose upon the retirement of an existing handler. There were two vacancies for the course starting on 23rd October 1978, and this was my goal.

Prior to my 1978 application I had had two previous applications to join the dog section denied. In 1974, when applications were invited, I duly applied and was rejected. The reason given was that as an officer with only two years' service, it was thought that my overall policing experience was inadequate. At this time it was considered that any new dog handler would generally require at least five years' experience as a police officer to adequately fill the role. One of the fundamental aspects of the job was that despite working as a team (man and dog), a dog handler worked with minimal supervision and as such you needed to be 'a bloody good copper' just to apply.

My second application was in late 1976 when I was on an eighteen-month secondment to the HQ CID Division Special Services Squad. This was a squad of twenty young, keen, ambitious officers who predominantly wanted to progress to the CID. We were thief-catchers in a covert, jeans-and-long-hair, undercover *Starsky & Hutch*-type squad.

When I applied I was hauled before the Deputy Commander of the entire Avon & Somerset CID, Detective Supt. Jack Everett. My application was rejected and he said something like this to me: "Why, lad, are you wasting our time? It is costing a fortune to train you up as a potential CID officer, now why on earth do you want to be a bloody dog walker? Get out of my office and forget all this nonsense!"

Then in around June 1978, when I was back in uniform at Trinity Road, I saw in force orders that applications were invited again for a dog course commencing in late October. As already stated, there were only forty dog handlers out of about 3,200 officers. Every time there were applications invited, I believe there were well over fifty applicants. The first task was getting through this initial paper sift, and to become one of the seven or eight that would get an interview. To this end you needed the endorsement of your section sergeant (Bert Barker, my old training school instructor) and more importantly that of your group inspector (in my case Inspector Eric Govier). Bert and Mr Govier were brilliant; they gave me their 100% support, although notwithstanding that, they said my loss to the group would be immense!

What did assist me in my application was quite a unique occurrence that came my way earlier in 1978. By this time, I was married to Linda and had two daughters: Janet, six, and Marie, two. Our third daughter Laura was due to arrive around mid-August. We had lived in a police house in North Bristol for a few years when the opportunity came to move two doors up into a house with a large corner plot garden. I was constantly thinking ahead, and to me, having a large garden would be an advantage when applying to become a dog handler.

We duly moved in about May 1978, and as soon as I got the green light to submit my application in around June I contacted an acquaintance in the police photographic department; I recall his name was Glynn. This budding civilian police photographer came to my house and with his wide-angle lens made the rear garden of my house look like ten acres of Longleat Safari Park. He neatly produced a set of pictures from all angles in a presentation folder that, excuse the pun, looked the dog's bollocks!

I think it was now about early July when Sgt Barker called me into the sergeant's office at Trinity Road and informed me that I had a time and date for my interview to become a dog handler.

Bert Barker advised me to prepare well for the interview, and to do everything in my power to be successful so that if I failed then it would be no fault of mine. It would simply be that a better man beat me on the day.

What I did next was a little unusual. I eventually got feedback from the interviewing panels and I was told that no one had completed an interview in quite that manner before. What I did was write out a speech that would answer the very first question: "Why do you want to be a dog handler?" The speech lasted about fourteen minutes; it even had bullet points which I expanded upon. The format of the speech went something like this:

- I have loved dogs from a very early age.
- Mum would not let me have one.
- The careers visit at school; seeing the police presentation.
- How at fourteen I decided that I wanted to be a dog handler.
- How as a cadet I worked with handlers at Kingsweston Sports Ground.
- How I applied with two years' services and was rejected.
- How on CID I applied and was rejected.
- How I moved house for a larger garden.
- I presented photographs of the garden.

- How most dog work was crime-centred, and apprehending criminals was my forte.
- How my inspector and sergeant were in full support.
- How I truly thought of this as my vocation in the police services.
- How nothing was more important to me in my police life than becoming a dog handler.
- It was all I had dreamt about since I was fourteen years old.
- No officer wanted this more than me!

As I entered the interview room I saw three senior officers sat at a table in front of me: Supt. Grundy (support services), Chief Inspector Skelland (personnel) and Inspector Langley (officer I/C of the dog section).

True to form, Supt. Grundy said to me, "Why do you want to be a dog handler and why should we choose you?"

Well, off I went on my fourteen-minute monologue whilst showing my portfolio of garden photos. I ploughed on until the very end and finished with, "I can assure you, no officer wants this more than me."

At the end there was silence. All of the officers looked at each other open-mouthed. Inspector Langley looked at me and said, "Thank you, Peter, you have answered every conceivable question we could ever have asked you. You will hear of our findings in due course."

During the interview another person had been present. There was a young lady, a secretary, who had been taking minutes for the benefit of the interview panel. Although I did not know this young lady, it transpired that she was the girlfriend of an officer who was on my group, but was stationed at Central. Later the following week he contacted me. He said that his girlfriend had said to him, "When Pete Chaplin left the interview room, the two senior officers turned to Inspector Langley and said, 'Brian, you've got to have him! His enthusiasm was unbelievable.'"

About three weeks later I had a bit of a bittersweet short memo from Supt. Grundy. It read:

Congratulations! You have been successful in your application to join the dog section. The course is due to commence on the 23rd of October. However, this may be delayed as at present we are having difficulty finding you a suitable dog.

Fantastic! Brilliant! Great news! Now, just find me a dog! They did find me a dog and that's a whole new story.

MY LIFE ON THE DOG SECTION BEGINS

I officially started as a police dog handler on Monday 23rd October 1978. A week or so prior to this I had been summoned to Bower Ashton by Sgt Ron Pell, who was going to be the instructor for my thirteen-week basic dog course. Ron had found me a 'suitable' German Shepherd for the course.

After a brief chat with Ron I went into the kennels where I had my first sighting of my German Shepherd bitch called Dena. Dena was a long-haired, rather small bitch with a beautiful face. She was the sort of Alsatian that you saw on those large boxes of Cadbury's chocolates at Christmas time. She honestly looked divine. Ron had a magnificent, huge, long-haired German Shepherd called Rinty. Rinty truly was a giant, and looked every bit the typical police dog.

A week went by and then I turned up on the Monday morning ready to start the course, getting in early to make a good impression. Having not seen Dena for a week, I was very excited to see her. On walking through the kennels from the car park I was amazed at what I saw. In Kennels 3 and 4 were the two new dogs for the course. In Kennel 3 was a nicely sized, short-haired GSD. The name *Shane* and the handler's name, *PC Poole*, were written in chalk on the board attached to the wire front of the kennel. PC Jeff Poole (an ex-traffic officer) was my fellow novice handler on day one. Then next door in Kennel 4 (which had the names *Dena* and *PC Chaplin*) was a phenomenal beast of a dog. I thought that she looked magnificent. I could not believe how much my Dena had grown in a week. I was so chuffed – from feeling somewhat inferior and a little disappointed with my Dena,

I was now deliriously happy! As you will shortly discover, however, this euphoria was short-lived.

The first hour was taken up with meeting the other handlers on the course and being issued with various items of kit and clothing. At about 10.30am Ron Pell told us to get our dogs on a lead in the top car park because we were going for a walk. I followed Ron into the kennels, where to my horror that fine, long-haired beast I saw earlier greeted Ron with yelps of joy – it was at that moment that I realised this mighty specimen of a dog was Ron's Rinty, and that my little Dena was behind the partition slide door, waiting nervously to be claimed. Ron took Rinty out and I pulled the wire loop that opens the separating door, and slowly and timidly my tiny little Dena appeared. She looked even smaller than the previous week – oh dear! I was not a happy bunny. However, at least I was on the dog section and I had to put 100% effort into making the next thirteen weeks with Dena as successful as possible.

Basic Police Dog Course
23rd October 1978–29th January 1979
Operational With Dena

I started on Sgt Brian Instone's group towards the end of January 1979. Initially, I covered the old D Division (St George & Lockleaze) areas of the city. The other handlers in our group were Howard Jones (A Division), Derek Gardner (B Division) and Tom Hornsby (C Division). For two weeks I was doubled up with Derek to learn the ropes.

Derek Gardner was a fantastic guy, only about 5'8" tall, and he had been a PTI in the army. He was as hard as nails and a very intelligent man. He had passed his sergeants' exam years ago; however, he had been constantly overlooked for promotion within the section due to his 'attitude problem'. Derek did not suffer fools gladly, and he was certainly not a yes-man. Consequently, the bosses didn't like him. Derek had done some boxing years earlier, the result of which was a wide, flat nose and nasal polyps (skin tabs in the nasal passages). This all meant that Derek quite literally had no sense of smell.

We were on a late turn covering B Division, Knowle West, Hartcliffe, etc. In those days we had old-shape Ford Escort vans with two dog cages in the back. I believe the late turn in those days was 5pm to midnight. Dena was in the cage behind the front passenger seat and Derek's dog Zimba was behind Derek, who was driving the van. Quite often the dogs would be barking loudly up against the metal partition that separated the cages. I have said before that Dena was small, probably about 65lbs. Zimba was quite small also, about 70lbs; however, I am sure that Zimba had alligator DNA in his makeup. He was 70lbs of gnashing, bone-crunching teeth. He was one of the most feared dogs on the section. What made him dangerous was that unlike most police dogs, who were trained to bite a leather protective sleeve and would do so, on a chase and attack exercise Zimba would probably bite the sleeve first, then come off and do you in the legs. Potentially a very dangerous and unpredictable dog.

It was a cold night and we had the van's heater on. From about 6.30pm I thought that I could smell dog shit in the rear of the van, but Derek made no comment (at this early stage I didn't know that Derek had no sense of smell). By 7pm, the smell was very bad and the heat from the van's heater was cooking the odour nicely. By 8pm, it was putridly disgusting and vile. I didn't like to say anything because Derek still had made no comment at all. I felt sick and I had to have the windows open; I wanted to throw up. At about 8.30pm we returned to Bower for our grub break. As we got into the yard and parked Brian Instone approached us and enquired as to the brown gas coming out of the van's roof vent. It was truly disgusting. Dena, probably upset by Zimba's barking, had shit repeatedly all over the inside of the cage. Over the next two hours she had laid in it, peed on it and generally recycled it all around the cage. Derek had not smelt a thing. What a great first tour of duty as a dog handler! We then had to spend the rest of the shift cleaning the van and Dena herself. There was no way on earth that I was putting a long-haired GSD covered in shit and piss in the back of my personal car to take home at the end of the shift.

I should have explained earlier that we were all issued with a large £1,000 wooden kennel that catered for our dogs at our home addresses. Our dogs lived with us 24/7, 365 days of the year.

Over the year we had a few bitches, and I do recall two in particular that were very good. Firstly, Elsa with Cyril Haddy, and later on, Ayesha with Paul Lowrie. Bitches do tend to be very maternal towards their handlers, and the bond between handler and dog is normally very strong. However, a good bitch is no better than a good dog, and a good dog is always bigger. I am not saying biggest is best; however, I was a 6' 1", fifteen-stone guy with a small 65lb bitch, which to be honest wasn't very good. Dena was a lovely little German Shepherd bitch, but unfortunately she was as useful as a chocolate teapot.

Dena was a reasonable tracker, and her quartering and searching skills were adequate. However, when it came to criminal/man work, her aggression and fear factor were quite poor. On the stick attack and steadiness to gun she was quite weak, plus she was scared of the dark. This was quite an obstacle to overcome considering that about 80% of our jobs were at night, during the hours of darkness.

We did, however, have a few successes together, but after less than twelve months Dena was retired from service. She went to live for many happy years as the family pet of the legendary traffic motorcyclist and ex-Royal Marine John Claridge and his family.

Knowing that Dena was retiring I had the difficult task of finding a replacement. We were being offered gift dogs all of the time. However, finding a suitable prospect was much easier said than done. For me, my requirements were as follows: a dog, not a bitch – no more bitches for me; aged ten to eighteen months; a bit of attitude/aggression and an overpowering desire to retrieve.

This desire to retrieve is absolutely paramount. A large amount of our dog training was centred around the dogs' desire to chase after a moving object (in the wild this would be his prey, his food and his survival), and to catch it and retrieve it.

Tracking, for example: you get someone to hold your dog, you walk off through the long grass waving his favourite toy or ball, and place his ball, say, fifty yards away from him at the end of your track in the grass. You then return to him on exactly the same track, display that you don't have his ball, and with the tracking harness fitted you encourage the dog to put his nose to the ground whilst saying the command, "Seek." Initially, because he wants to retrieve his ball, he just charges out the fifty yards until he finds the ball. This process is repeated and repeated, time after time, until one day the penny drops and the dog realises that if he follows the ground scent disturbance he will find his ball. It's then time to increase the time and distance of the track. Eventually, when you put the tracking harness on the dog it will automatically put its nose to the ground and begin sniffing for a scent. All of this exercise is dependent on the dog wanting to retrieve or fetch the ball. If the dog has no desire to retrieve, then he won't show any interest when you return and put the tracking harness on. It will be a waste of time!

One of my tests that I used to give a potential police gift dog would be to take the dog and his favourite toy to a piece of ground where there was a bramble bush. I would tease the dog by pretending time after time to go to throw the ball, but would not let go of it. The dog hopefully would become excited and start barking, eager for me to throw his ball. It was then, hopefully after the dog had barked, that I would throw his ball into the middle of the bramble bush. I was looking for a loony dog who just leapt into the brambles without a care – a dog who literally didn't give a shit about the thorns. His only thought was to get his ball no matter what!

It was the same story with quartering. This means searching an area of open ground or a building for a hidden criminal. What happens is that the dog is on its lead, held by you, and another handler teases him with his ball and then runs off with it out of sight. The dog is barking because he wants his ball. After a short while you run into the building with the dog on its lead, keen to retrieve his ball, then you go a short distance and find the handler, who is tossing the ball up in the air. The dog is excited; he barks and is rewarded with his ball. He has retrieved it. Gradually the distance is increased and the handler begins to conceal himself.

Eventually, the handler is totally concealed and the dog searches and locates him purely on air scent. The point here is that the dog has the desire to retrieve, and that is what gives him the keenness to search for the man who might have his ball.

With my police dog Major, he initially had the strong desire to retrieve. However, as he matured his desire to bite and attack became the overriding reason for searching and tracking anyone. I think in his mind was, I can't bite 'em till I find 'em, so I need to be an excellent tracker/quarterer – which he was!

In around 1979, I visited Marie and George T at their home in Kingswood, Bristol. They had an eleven-month-old GSD by the name of Major. They had had him since ten weeks of age, and their problem was that Major had growled twice at their grandson.

They lived in a built-up area and I didn't have the time or space to try a retrieval test. However, he was a good size, black and tan GSD who certainly looked the part. His pedigree showed that on one line he had the 'Joda' bloodline; I was told later by a GSD breeder that this was an excellent working dog line.

I took him on test for a week to see how he went. The following day I had to attend court and another handler, Neil Barnes, agreed to take him out to see if he could get him retrieving. I got back to Bower Ashton about midday and Barnsey shouted to me, "Bloody hell, Pete, your Major retrieves fantastically – he'd run through a brick wall to get his ball!" Fantastic news – I now had my dog! However, little did I know that he was going to go on and become a bit of a legend in his own right.

It didn't take me long to realise that within the dog section there were basically four types of dogs and handlers.

1. Trials dogs and handlers: these were teams (dog and man) that were trained up to the highest possible standard. The dogs were competent at every exercise. They competed every year at regional dog trials and regularly qualified for the national police dog trials. Avon & Somerset had national winners in

Bob Forsyth (Somerset & Bath), Jeff Poole, I believe, and Andy Lloyd. These handlers were at the top of their profession, but not necessarily the best operational handlers. Other exceptional dog trainers were the likes of Dick Burton, Pete Richards, Paul Lowrie, Ron Pell, Brian Instone, Bob Forsyth and Vernon Essex. I must emphasise that these guys did not get there by luck. Yes, they had amazing natural talent but they also put in the hours and hours of repetitive training that enabled their gifted animals to attain the highest standards possible.

2. The second type of handlers and dogs were of this very high standard but could also do it on the street, bringing in prisoners through great dog work. Truly only one springs to mind – this is a very rare breed indeed – but in my books Andy Lloyd was just such a handler. Possibly the best dog trainer I have ever seen, plus an excellent street dog handler. Andy's commitment to his training and his dogs was second to none.

3. The third type, and I would like to include myself in this category, are average dog trainers (in my case probably just below average training ability). However, this group were bloody good coppers and thief-catchers. Within this group I consider myself in the top ten. I was enthusiastic, tenacious, patient and had a never-give-up mentality. The number of times I would stay at a job for maybe an hour, sitting quiet, waiting for the villains who had gone to ground to re-emerge. I had 508 prisoners in my twenty years. However, the daddy of this group was a fantastic guy by the name of Pete Temlett, whose original dog was Monty. Pete, based at Weston-super-Mare, was six feet tall and fifteen stone of sheer muscle. He worked out daily, had a superb physique; was as hard as nails and totally fearless. He was a former electrical officer on the *QE2*, but believe me, he should have been in the special forces, he was that good. In my humble opinion he was one of, if not the best policeman with a dog I have ever worked with. Not wishing to sound conceited, I was pretty good but Pete (Wally) Temlett left me standing. Other good handlers in this

category were the likes of Trevor Smith, Bob Lonsdale, Pete Bush, Clive 'Willis' Dunster, Tony Corkell, Paul Bath, Ian Shutt, Paul Rocket, Norman Stephenson, Ray Holmes, Jimbo Watts, Steve Hathway and Neil Dale. A special mention must go to another Weston dog handler, Dave Sirell, originally from Brighton. Dave was a slim, wiry-haired human dynamo. Like Pete Temlett he was fearless and formidable. Not wishing to upset anyone by not giving them a mention, the majority of handlers fell into this Group 3 category. I must further explain that my thoughts are predominately around the years 1978 to 1998. I fully appreciate that the original handlers, Tom Hornsby and Derek Johnson, were legends; likewise Alan Matthews, Terry Connell, Cyril Haddy, Bob Sevier, Norman Oliver, Father Ball and the like.

4. The final category is for the handlers who were like me: not particularly good dog trainers but who were 110% out-and-out great thief-catchers, and who simply were, with the addition of a police dog, even better thief-catchers.

In hindsight, perhaps I should have classified myself in this group; after all, I had never qualified in the top eight at the force internal trials, yet I was a bloody good dog handler.

Please understand that everything I have said is purely my own opinion, and no one else's.

LIST OF MY DOGS AND BRIEF COMMENTS ON EACH

In my twenty years on dogs I had a total of nine canine companions; ten if you take into account the six weeks that I had a very excitable Doberman by the name of Zeus. Of these, eight were general purpose police dogs and two were specialist 'explosive search dogs'.

The dogs were as follows:

German Shepherd – Dena
65lbs, Bitch, 23rd October 1978–12th December 1979

Dena was my first police dog. She was petite and lovely (I often later referred to her as the Canine Lady) and she went on to finally make a wonderful family pet in 1990. Not very suitable as a police dog. She was nervous and did not like the dark or man work. I was quite relieved when the decision was made to replace her.

German Shepherd – Major
95lbs, Dog, 17th September 1979–13th August 1984

What can I say? This dog really was the business! An amazing animal, great tracker and searcher. He was fearless and totally formidable. His forte was man work (biting), and all he really wanted to do was attack things – people preferably, but he would also bite chairs, lampposts, phone boxes, doors – anything, in fact. Because he wanted to attack, he would track or search in order to get in a position to bite.

Died in my arms, put to sleep on 13th August 1984.

German Shepherd – Jake
80lbs, Dog, 3rd September 1984–20th September 1986

Jake was a good-looking, long-haired GSD. He was of average build with a good temperament, but compared to Major he was decidedly average. Sadly, Jake broke his back when he fell awkwardly off a wall on a job in Clifton. He was put to sleep on 20th September 1986.

English Springer Spaniel – Sammy the Seagull
Dog, 23rd February 1985–4th August 1986

Sammy was my first specialist search dog trained to detect explosives. He was very good indeed, until, that is, this incident occurred which resulted in two things: 1) he got his nickname of Sammy the Seagull, and 2) he ended up limping as a three-legged dog for the rest of his days.

One day (and he had never done this before) whilst we were conducting an external explosive search near to Bower Ashton, he took notice of a very low-flying seagull. Off Sammy charged, pursuing the gull at speed. No amount of commands or calls would stop him. He had developed selective deafness for these few seconds. Then the inevitable happened: Sammy ran down a small lane, out of the wood and straight out onto the road, where he collided with a passing car. The end result, after a lengthy visit to the vet, was that he carried one of his hind legs constantly. Believe it or not he still searched well; however, it was eventually decided to retire Sammy to a farm in the Chew Valley in Somerset. We could not have a three-legged spaniel on operational duty – it would look bad for the constabulary. Last I heard of Sammy was in about 1990, when I heard that in addition to seagulls he was now chasing rooks, crows and pigeons.

Black Labrador – Samson the Loony Lab
Dog, 4th April 1986–9th July 1987

Samson was a loony bomb dog. His mind was basically preoccupied with two things: sex and food. I am not going to dwell on Samson, as his story is one of those that I am not at liberty to divulge.

German Shepherd – Defer
105lbs, Dog, 23rd September 1986–3rd October 1990

This dog was a gift dog from a family in Stroud in Gloucestershire. His name had already been given to him: Defer, as in 'D for dog'. He was a big, masculine, tough dog; a typical police dog. A reasonable tracker and searcher with an extremely hard bite, unfortunately Defer retired early due to illness.

German Shepherd – Major II
100lbs, Dog, 3rd October 1990–5th March 1991

Not to be confused with Major (The Beast); however, similar in appearance and attitude to a degree. The only thing I did not like about this dog was his lack of honesty. When you were playing the part of a criminal (i.e. a dog handler wearing a leather sleeve) and you ran for Major II, sometimes after biting the sleeve he would let you go and then bite your leg or ass. Not very nice; not very honest. I was quite pleased in March 1991 when Vernon Essex (the sergeant on dogs) suggested that we swap dogs. He had a very nice run-of-the-mill dog called Justice, who was not tasty enough for him. Truly, after my recent experiences with Major II I was quite happy to opt for a quieter life. Justice became Jason 6th March 1991.

German Shepherd – Jason
75lbs, Dog, 6th March 1991–19th September 1998

Jason was an average police dog. He got all his courage from me and on a few occasions I sent him to detain criminals. He would go out of sight, and usually the villain got away. This was in such contrast to Major, because I knew if I sent him to chase and detain an offender then it was nearly always mission accomplished. Straight to A&E at the Bristol Royal Infirmary, do not pass Go, do not collect £200! Locating your prisoner was easy; it was simply a case of following the blood-curdling screams.

Jason was safe – a reasonable tracker and searcher, but not the dog you would take with you to the Alamo to fight alongside Davy Crockett and Jim Bowie.

German Shepherd Puppy – Zak

This will be the final story in Book 2 – *More Job, Less Bite* – so more on that then.

DOG BITES THAT I RECEIVED

'A job with bite' it certainly is. If you are not prepared to get bitten occasionally, if you are not prepared to get hurt, not prepared for your skin to get pinched and then get hurt again, then don't become a dog handler.

In my twenty years on the section, Major dished out a few bites. Mostly to fleeing criminals, some to police officers and a few to innocent members of the public who simply got in the way. But these next pages are a personal record of how yours truly, Pete Chaplin, suffered grief and pain at the hand of 'man's best friend'.

My first experience of getting bitten by a police dog was in 1971 when I was a police cadet at the Bristol Constabulary Sports Ground, which was at Kingsweston near to Blaise Castle in North Bristol. The sports field was a popular place for Bristol handlers to train with their dogs.

Now, although this was forty-four years ago I can still recall the fear, the anxiety, the trepidation and then the pressure and pain of that first dog bite. Yes, I was wearing that thick leather purpose-built dog sleeve and yes, it bloody hurt! I'm not too sure if it was John Carpenter or Father Ball who was the handler, but the dog's name, Smokey, rings a bell.

Joining the section in 1978 and being on a basic course of seven dogs ensured that I duly received my fair share of dog bites from the other novice dogs on the course. I have mentioned the leather dog sleeves that were predominately used, but for really hard-biting dogs you could have leather liner inserts to increase protection. However, in addition to leather sleeves we also used crepe bandages wrapped around the forearm for protection. The bandages were used for two main reasons:

1. On a basic course with baby dogs it could be useful to introduce the dogs to biting something a little softer, not as hard as a leather sleeve. This is obviously dependent on the dog – some, like Major, took to biting instinctively but others required coaxing and bandages can be the answer.
2. Bandages are great to use under old coats. You can't wear a sleeve under a coat; however, layers and layers of bandages can achieve protection and the covert solution required. Wearing bandages for the first time is very daunting. As the dog is bearing down on you, you start to think, Have I put enough bandages on?

Bandages certainly are the preferred choice when training dogs not to become sleeve-orientated. The negative things with bandages are that they take time to apply and you get through old coats very quickly because they soon get ripped to shreds. The benefits of a dog sleeve are that they are quickly fitted and nearly all dogs love biting a sleeve.

Let's not kid ourselves, all dog bites hurt to a degree. Sometimes those little front teeth-pinchers on bandages can be quite painful.

Early on in my dog career I had the misfortune to run for Bender Barnes and his old dog Sabre. Neil and I joined as cadets in 1970. He was on the section a few years before me and has gone on to bigger and better dog jobs all over the world. Neil had taken over a dog from an older handler, Des Flood, who had left the section. The piss-take with Bender was that people would wind him up by saying, "Dessie's dog" to him all the time. Well, Dessie's dog or not, when Sabre bit me that first time it was excruciating. On my life, it was like getting bitten by a huge saltwater crocodile. I used the comparison of a salty because from what I have read and seen of them on the telly they truly are fearsome predators (just like old Sabre was).

Another bite that I sustained early in my dog career, and for which

I still carry the scar now on the second finger of my right hand, was down to Brian Instone's dog, which I believe was called Rebel.

Brian had transferred down on promotion to sergeant from Stockton-on-Tees, Middlesbrough in Cleveland. His dog Rebel was a nice dog, a really nice dog – that was the problem. I think that sometimes the best police dogs are those with an edge. Those who are a little suspicious of folk, those who would not let anyone approach the van without barking their head off. Those that have the German Shepherd 'I am guarding my sheep' mentality. I sometimes think that my Major's DNA was a cross between that of a Tyrannosaurus Rex and the Hound of the Baskervilles.

We needed to very gently encourage Rebel to be less people-friendly. The simple action plan was for people to approach Rebel in a nice, friendly manner, smoothing him lovingly, talking to him nicely and then suddenly slap him across his snout (but not too hard). At first this did not seem to work. Upon being slapped across the nose Rebel used to simply blink and wag his tail.

I tried again, with the same result. No retaliation or aggression from Rebel whatsoever. I slapped his snout over and over again, and then complacency set in on my part. After constant ignorance of all my snout-slapping, Rebel all at once thought enough was enough, and on my next attempt I didn't even get close to his nose. Before I made contact, he growled and bit my hand; my second finger on my right hand was ripped open to the bone. The three-inch scar is still there today, over thirty-five years later. Rebel never looked back, and I think that I was the making of that dog.

I have mentioned Derek Gardner before; a good friend of mine and great dog handler. Derek had a fearsome dog by the name of Zimba. Zimba was quite small in comparison to other GSDs on the section; however, although probably only 70lbs in weight, Zimba was 70lbs of venom, terror and sheer unpredictability.

As the new kid on the block I was the only one naive enough to run for Zimba. The trick was to always run with a sleeve on each arm, and be aware that after biting the sleeve, Zimba would invariably let go of the sleeve and then bite you in the legs. You had to be very quick, readjusting the sleeves to protect your lower limbs. Once or twice I did get a nip on the bum, but nothing too serious.

The next little tale involves a very close shave indeed. In the early 80s there was a guy in our group called Howard Jones. He was an experienced handler on his second dog. Howard had just completed his latest basic course with his new dog Lucky (what a name!). It was a late turn and we had met up at a small industrial estate in Whitehall, Bristol. This was not supposed to be biting criminal work. This was open quartering, basically hide and seek. What would happen was that out of sight of Howard's dog, I would make off into the industrial estate and hide. Sometimes accessible, sometimes inaccessible; I would not be wearing a sleeve (as this might encourage the dog to bite), but sometimes, if it was a tasty or unpredictable dog, you might wear one, just to be on the safe side.

In theory, the dog is released to find you, using the wind and airborne scent; the dog hopefully hones in on your scent and after locating you, barks to tell his handler that the person has been located. Sometimes this person could be a criminal or an elderly missing person, or maybe a vulnerable child. The point is that you do not want that eighty-year-old pensioner with dementia who's been missing for eight hours to be savaged by an overzealous police dog after being found.

So there we were in this industrial estate in Bristol, and Lucky was looking for me. I was stood in a dark outside corner of a single-storey building at the far end of the estate. I'd chosen the position well, as I could see when the dog was approaching, which gave me a few seconds to consider my actions if the approaching dog appeared too aggressive or threatening.

I suddenly saw Lucky approaching, and fortunately Howard was not far behind him. The dog quickly got a trace of my scent and it wasn't long before he was closing in on me. However, what happened next was a little frightening and disconcerting. Lucky was quite a large, mature dog, and as he closed in on me he started to bark, which is fine, but then he began jumping up and trying to nip me in the face. I was shitting myself, and Howard was shouting, "No, no, Lucky, no!" At the same time, he was yelling to me, "Next time he jumps up, knee him in his chest." I thought, Bugger that, I'm asking to get bitten!

This fiasco carried on for about thirty seconds until Howard was close enough to prevent Lucky jumping. Well, I'm telling you, I was not impressed. Howard afterwards explained that Lucky did have a tendency to jump and go for your face. Well, thanks very much for telling me! Howard was a lovely bloke; however, I didn't do many quarters for Lucky after this episode.

The last story in this little section is about the time I was bitten full-on by my operational police dog Defer.

Defer was a big, typical police dog. When this incident occurred I think Defer was approaching six years of age. He had been a police dog for about four years and had a hard, firm bite.

Defer had in fact been unwell, and unbeknown to me at this time he was suffering from liver cancer, which I later understood seriously affected his behaviour and temperament. We were still awaiting veterinary lab test results on Defer, and contingency plans were in hand to replace him if necessary. I had tried a couple of dogs in recent weeks, and I now had a young GSD by the name of Frankie in provisional training.

Frankie had been living at home in the same kennel as Defer. They got on fine. Frankie understood the pack order and was submissive to Defer, who ruled the roost. The two of them together were no problem.

On the day in question I was up on Purdown with my colleague from Weston, a true legend of a dog handler called Pete Temlett. He had his new dog out running with my two and there were no problems.

The three dogs had been running and playing quite nicely for a fair time when all of a sudden and for no reason Defer viciously attacked Frankie. Poor old Frankie did not know what hit him. He was on his back, ears flat in submission and Defer was ripping at his throat, growling very aggressively. There was a lot of blood (all Frankie's) and bits of fur flying everywhere.

Pete had grabbed his dog and I was struggling to get Defer off of Frankie. I gave Defer a few clouts after screaming at him to "Leave! Leave!" Eventually he let go, and Frankie ran off about thirty yards, whimpering, whining and bleeding.

I laugh now, as Pete was shouting loudly, "Don't panic! Don't panic!" just like Corporal Jones out of *Dad's Army*. Believe it or not, this was not the end. I bellowed at Defer to go into the 'down' position, which he did, about six feet in front of me. Then almost immediately and without warning, Defer's eyes seemed to turn green and he attacked me. He gave me a full-on vice-like bite on my right arm. Three of his canines went into my flesh and one scraped the outside of my arm.

I instinctively screamed, "No! No! Leave!" and he instantly released and looked at me as if to say, "Oops, what have I done?"

Defer was quickly put in one cage of the van and I managed to get Frankie in the other cage. Frankie had some superficial wounds to his neck, which bled a bit and probably looked worse than they were. He was later repaired at our vets in Nailsea.

Looking at my own injuries I could see three distinct holes in my arms: two puncture wounds and a larger wound that in fact had a lump of my fatty tissue sticking out of it. Amazingly at the time of the attack I felt nothing, but now, however, I was feeling a little sick and dizzy. We jiggled the vans around and Pete took me to Southmead A&E.

Upon arrival at A&E I think they gave me another tetanus booster and cleaned my wounds. When the staff nurse was seeing to the largest wound she said, "Just as well we got this out", and to my horror she removed a clump of dog fur from Frankie's throat that had been inside my arm. She then duly poked the lump of tissue back into the hole. Goodness knows what problems I would have had if that had stayed inside my arm! Within twelve hours my right arm looked like Popeye's, and I was in agony.

Dog bites? Yeah, I've had a few!

THE UNIQUE MAJOR RELEASE TECHNIQUE

There was the odd occasion when Major had bitten someone and he could be reluctant to release them. The technique usually involved a bit of yelling on behalf of the criminal, a bit of growling on behalf of Major and bit of shouting, "Major, leave!" on behalf of me. To help facilitate the release I used to nibble on one of his ears and tickle his goolies. This always had the desired effect, and release was almost instantaneous. A little bit like the Heimlich manoeuvre without the toffee stuck in the throat!

FUNNY STORIES AT BOWER ASHTON

During my twenty years on the section there were many amusing little incidents that occurred. I have included a few below.

Not So Fast

In early 1979 I was the new kid on the block, just off the basic course and raring to impress. As a group, on days we were up on the plateau in Ashton Court Estate, about a mile up from the Mounted & Dog HQ at Bower Ashton. One of the guys on my group was Tom Hornsby. Tom was one of the original two handlers that formed the Bristol Constabulary Dog Section in 1957. The other officer was the legendary Derek Johnson.

Tom was a mate of the section Inspector Brian Langley, and both Tom and his dog (coincidentally named Major) were getting on a bit. I reckon that Tom was nearing sixty and Major was well over ten years old. Major was the oldest-looking police dog I had ever seen; his muzzle was completely grey and he should have had a canine Zimmer frame. Both Tom and his dog were cruising down the last few months until their respective retirements.

On this particular afternoon, I can't recall why but Sgt Ron Pell, and not our group Sgt Brian Instone, was taking the training and he told me to put on a dog sleeve and do a quick chase and attack for Tom and Major.

I was new and did not understand or appreciate that Tom's participation in training was quite minimal, and certainly not full-on. I only learned later that any chase and attacks these two participated in were very short in distance and slow in pace.

Well, off I zoomed at a fair rate of knots; I was about seventy yards ahead of Tom to begin with and I was running like the wind.

I ran as fast as I could with my sleeve arm hanging invitingly out to my right-hand side, and I did not look behind me at all, but was conscious that at any moment that 100lbs of snarling GSD would latch onto my arm and I would be lucky to stay on my feet.

As the new boy I was anxious not to appear hesitant or afraid in any way. I ran and ran and waited, but nothing.

Then shouts and whistles rang out, and I came to a stop and glanced behind me. As I turned around I saw Tom's dog Major collapsed on the grass about seventy yards behind me. A further sixty to seventy yards behind the dog was the prone figure of Tom, also collapsed and motionless on the grass.

I hurriedly rejoined the other lads who had congregated around Tom and discovered that what had happened was that as I zoomed off, Tom released Major, who initially started chasing me at a reasonable pace, but then slowed down and soon collapsed. Tom, meanwhile, had started jogging after his dog at a slow pace, but then had also collapsed about the same time as his dog.

Initially things looked quite serious for Tom; everyone thought that he had had a heart attack, and that his dog was dead. However, fortunately within fifteen minutes both man and dog were sat up and back in the land of the living.

For my trouble I got a bollocking from Ron for being too enthusiastic and running too fast, and needless to say this was the last chase and attack that Tom and his dog ever performed.

Brian Instone and the Sapling

Shortly after joining Brian Instone's group I found myself on a day's training in dense woodland at the far end of Long Ashton. I was the newest member of the group and with me that day were Mike Sheppard and yet another Rebel, Norman Stephenson and Sacha and Derek Gardner and the 'mini alligator' that was Zimba.

We were engaged on open quartering (hide and seek), and Brian was the sergeant instructor. One particular location we found was in quite a steep, wooded valley, and from the top you could look down into the valley floor and quite easily view where the criminal was hiding. Brian instructed Mike Shep to go next, and he told him to wait for five minutes whilst he made his way to the valley floor and hid up.

At this time Rebel, although a young dog, was a tough beast, but he was honest and would not nip a handler who was hiding in the open. Brian knew this, and we could see him happily stood by a young sapling about eighty yards down in the valley. Brian was merrily puffing away on a cigarette awaiting Mike's challenge. (You always gave a challenge when searching for a hidden criminal. It gave a real villain the opportunity to surrender, and in training it warned the handler who was hiding up to get prepared because a dog would soon be in his vicinity.) Bearing in mind that Brian was exposed and expecting Mike's challenge, what happened next was hilarious.

Rebel was going to be released, but as a windup Derek shouted out the challenge. Now Derek's voice was very deep and nasal, totally different to Mike's voice and immediately identifiable. Well, on hearing Derek's shout Brian almost shit himself; the expression on his face was one of sheer terror. His fag went flying. He had been expecting Rebel, but now the unthinkable was heading towards him! In his mind the alligator that was Zimba was on his way, and he had no time and nowhere to hide in safety. He was frantic, and did not know what to do for the best. There were no climbable trees within a safe distance, no possibility of sanctuary anywhere – he was f****d.

We viewed all of this from above just as Rebel was searching his way down the valley's side. Glancing back down at Brian, we saw a sight of pure slapstick comedy. In sheer desperation and blind panic, we saw Brian attempt to climb the small, thin, ten-foot sapling that he had been stood next to. He succeeded to a degree, but then the ultra slim sapling trunk bent double, and although probably eight feet up the trunk, Brian was now virtually hanging upside down with his head about eighteen inches off of the ground. We were all wetting ourselves, and when Derek shouted, "Where is he?" we knew that Brian was just bricking it.

The really funny bit then was when Rebel found the upside-down Brian and began barking in his face with no attempt whatsoever to nip him.

This was in 1979, long before mobile phones and cameras, otherwise £250 from *You've Been Framed* could have been winging its way to Bower Ashton.

Rumour has it that after this little escapade Brian always carried a spare pair of underpants in his kit bag – just in case?

He Did Not Enjoy the Trip

Once again, this little tale involves Tom Hornsby. On this occasion we were on a training day laying grass tracks at the far end of Avonmouth, near to the village of Hallen. This is only a few miles from the coastline of the Bristol Channel. The fields we were using to track in were bordered on one side by the London to South Wales railway line.

I was laying a track for Tom and I made it quite a basic eleven or twelve-leg affair, within two fields, and the end article was his dog's rubber ball. This was positioned about twenty yards from the far edge of the field. This side of the field had a wire fence boundary, and beyond that the thirty-foot-high railway embankment.

As I finished laying the track I walked up towards the wire fence, and to my horror I saw that my only way out of the field was across a ten-foot-wide flooded ditch. I had no option, as to have walked back across the field would have knackered the track.

This aquatic barrier was not very pleasant; it was covered in a green algae-type slime, and it stank. There were two factors which made breaching this ditch particularly hazardous. Firstly, on its far side and forming the boundary of the field were a number of concrete posts which had thin, rusted wire threaded through them. This meant that when you leapt across the ditch you had to grasp hold of the wire or risk falling backwards and into the three to four-foot deep, pongy water. The second potential hazard was that on the take-off side of the ditch there was a mass of overgrown briar and bramble bushes. These briars and brambles had long strands or runners, each possessing dozens of razor-sharp thorns.

I quickly assessed how I intended to jump across the water, and after a long, fast run-up, I sprang like a gazelle across the gap. On landing on the other side I grabbed the rusty, thin wire and prayed that it did not break. Thankfully it held my weight and I quickly scrambled through the wire and up the railway embankment where I sat and rested.

From where I was sat at the top of the railway embankment I could clearly see across the fields to where the dog vans were parked, and the start of Tom's track. After about thirty minutes I saw Tom get out of the van; he then got his dog Major out of the van's cage and proceeded to harness him up. Within a minute he was in the first field casting around the square to locate his start, and a few minutes later he was on, and away tracking.

Because of their ages, Tom and Major were tracking steadily but quite slowly. Around this time, I was joined up on the embankment by Sgt Brian Instone (group sergeant and instructor). Brian had been taking advantage of the elevated position up on the embankment to keep an eye on a few dogs who were tracking in adjacent fields. Tom was about halfway around his track when Brian joined me. Major was doing well, and Brian and I watched as Major completed his track and located the last article (his rubber ball). Tom unharnessed the dog, and to reward him for a successful track, he threw the ball out into the centre of the field a few times for the dog to chase and retrieve. Tom, meanwhile, was tidying up his harness and tracking line.

It was then time for Tom to determine the best way to exit the field and make his way back to the vans. He put Major in the down position and walked over to examine the flooded ditch. Now hindsight is a great thing, and perhaps he should have considered the mile walk back across the fields. However, with Brian and me looking down on him from the embankment, pride being what it is, and not wishing to lose face, Tom elected to jump.

As we looked down on Tom, he was a picture of intense concentration. He walked about ten paces back and then waited, breathing slowly and heavily. With one last deep breath he was off! He reminded me of Evel Knievel as he hurtled towards his attempted jump across the Grand Canyon, although in all fairness Tom was nowhere near as speedy. He was like a lumbering jumbo jet, slowly making its way down the runway at Heathrow (that's when you think, will this huge plane ever get off of the ground?). In all honesty Tom's approach was not particularly fast, and even at this early stage in the process I was starting to have my doubts about whether Tom would clear the water jump or not.

For a millisecond things appeared to be going OK – but then disaster struck! With the penultimate stride of his run-up and with his left foot actually airborne, his right boot got snagged on one of those trailing bramble runners which acted like nature's tripwires. This halted Tom's momentum dramatically. Everything now appeared as if in slow motion. Tom seemed to halt in mid-air, suspended in time, then *SPLOOSH* – the most impressive bellyflop I had ever witnessed, as gravity and Tom's weight succumbed to inevitability. The resulting splash into the murky gunge was spectacular. The water displacement reminded me very much of those classic scenes from the World War II film *The Dam Busters*.

Tom's quite considerable frame disappeared under the surface for a split second, only to reappear gasping for breath and spitting out copious amounts of ditch water. Tommy boy was not a happy bunny.

Up on the embankment Brian and I were wetting ourselves as we watched Tom drag himself to the far bank of the ditch. His language was bluer that the colour of his training suit, which incidentally was now covered in a smelly green gunge courtesy of his dip. Now just to add insult to injury, when Tom put Major into the sit position and then called the dog to join him, Major simply ran and jumped into the slimy gunge, and like his handler he was instantly changed from a black and tan GSD to a green GSD.

It was a very wet, smelly and sorry-looking dog team that made their way make to Bower to clean up and lick their wounds.

The unwarranted suggestion going around the section was that within a few months I had first tried to give Tom a heart attack up on the plateau in Ashton Court, and then I had tried to drown him at Hallen.

Within a few weeks Tom had actually retired, and ironically enough his retirement do was at the Ashton Court Mansion (all arranged by the section's good friend Pete Brown).

The Final Christmas Lunch Party

During the early 80s it somehow became a festive tradition at Bower Ashton to have a turkey dinner on probably the last Thursday or Friday before Christmas. The dog day group and day mounted officers attended, as well as occasional guys on leave days or whatever. The chief inspector and the inspector would attend, and perhaps a senior officer from HQ down at Old Bridewell. Up until now the Christmas meal had been quite a nice lunch, made by our cook in the canteen. On this particular lunchtime the guest from Force HQ was a female superintendent by the name of Terri Grundy. Miss Grundy was the senior officer on my dog section interview board back in 1978.

The cooking of the dinner was progressing nicely; the sprouts were coming to the boil and the Christmas pud was looking good. Supt Grundy had arrived and I presumed she was enjoying a pre-dinner sherry with Mr Cheetham and Mr Langley in the boss's office.

We, 'the horde', were milling around the main table waiting for the off. At the head of the long table was the VIP section; two smaller tables to sit four people. The configuration of the dining tables was like a long letter T.

Then to my horror I saw a dog handler take the salt cellar and remove the lid. He took it to the sugar basin on the top table, poured the contents into the sugar and stirred. He then half-filled the empty salt cellar with salt from the second cruet set on the long table. The perpetrator is no longer with us, unfortunately. Oh dear! I was thinking.

The top table was going to be Supt Grundy, Chief Inspector Cheetham, Inspector Langley and Gerry Haskey, the mounted supervisory.

Within fifteen minutes about twenty of us were sat at the table, pulling crackers, wearing paper hats and waiting for the tomato soup to be served. The top table was fully occupied and there was a buzz with gossip and chatter.

The soup arrived and it was delicious. Turkey and trimmings were next and were very nice (could have done with a few more roast potatoes, but I wasn't complaining). Then it was the Christmas pudding and custard, which was not bad at all.

After a pause at the end of dessert, the plates of mince pies and cups and saucers were arranged on all tables. Tea or coffee would soon be available. Sugar, anyone?

Before the pots of tea and coffee arrived, it was very noticeable that lots of dog handlers were leaving to either go to the loo, stretch their legs, give their dogs a run or head for the nearest bunker. All the mounted officers were blissfully ignorant and oblivious to the forthcoming explosion.

Supt Grundy opted for coffee and yes, you guessed it, she liked two spoons of sugar in her Nescafe. Well, one swig of coffee and a mouthful of salty Nescafe sprayed all over the table. Chaos immediately followed. She was Queen Victoria all over again: "We are not amused!" No more Christmas lunches, and a bollocking all round.

Norman's Wound

One summer afternoon we were on a training day and my good friend Norman Stephenson (a Geordie dog handler based in Bath) was playing the criminal as we completed a follow-on track in the vicinity of the Long Ashton bypass. Vernon Essex was sergeant in command. A follow-on track is where one handler runs off, say, fifteen minutes ahead of the others (maybe three or four handlers and dogs). He is in effect laying the track that all four dogs will follow in turn. In practice this track can go on for a few miles. Invariably what happens is that the handler laying the track tires, and quite often dog three or four will catch up with him.

This was the final leg of the track, and Vernon Essex and his dog (yet another Sacha) had caught up with Norman just as Norman was traversing an under-road water culvert, about halfway along the Long Ashton bypass. This culvert was a four-foot-wide concrete pipe which carried rainwater under the road, about sixty yards in length. Norman was about halfway through it, doing his best to manoeuvre through the pipe in a crouched position, shuffling along and trying not to kneel down in the three or four inches of running water that was flowing through the culvert.

Suddenly, Vernon was at the other end of the culvert. His dog Sacha, upon seeing and smelling Norman, became very excited and started barking. Norman tried to speed up, but as a big and heavy man, he was tired.

Then disaster struck (well, as far as Norman was concerned). Because the tracking line was wet and slippery, and because Sacha was excited and pulling hard, Vernon lost his grip on the nylon rope line. He dropped it and Sacha was now making a beeline straight for Norman's ass. Like a laser-guided missile, Sacha homed in with pinpoint accuracy.

The sounds in the culvert were very confusing; the acoustics outrageous. Barks and yelps and calls of "Leave! Leave! Sacha! No! No!" were bouncing off of the culvert's walls. The first confirmation for Norman that he had been caught was when he felt the searing pain of Sacha's teeth munching on his buttocks. Then he banged his head on the roof of the culvert. Then Vernon had the line and was trying to pull the dog off; then Norman banged his head again. All in all, for Norman this was just another fun-filled day in paradise.

Forwarding on thirty minutes, and we are in the main office at Bower Ashton. Norman is bemoaning his fate, and with the first aid box located we have to decide if Norman requires hospital treatment. Bearing in mind the location of the wound, Norman is literally not in a position to view the injury to make any logical decision upon the treatment required. In steps the highly qualified Médecins Sans Frontières, Florence Nightingale type, Betty Hookway. Betty was a sixty-five-year-old chain-smoking short-sighted secretary who ran Bower Ashton. As the only female, sympathetic person in sight, Norman sought her advice and guidance.

"Drop yer trousers, lovey, I've seen it all before," she bellowed.

Upon him doing as requested, Betty examined Norman's buttock for quite a few seconds. Glasses on and then glasses off. Then with a deep intake of breath she exclaimed, "That definitely needs a stitch, Norman."

Quick as a flash, Bob Lonsdale chipped in: "Betty, you're looking at his asshole – the dog bite is about three inches to the right!" Well, that was it – we all collapsed in laughter. Norman had a plaster stuck on his wound and off he went, home to bathe.

Remember – they don't stitch dog bites!

Dinsey's Dilemma

We were coming to the end of a night shift. It was about 5.15am and Bob Lonsdale (also known as Dinsey) and I were parked up on Brandon Hill off Park Street in Bristol. This was a great location, as you could give your dogs a run up and down the very steep hill that goes from the lake by the tower down in the direction of Great George Street.

Standing at the top, you could throw your dog's ball on a rope a long, long way. The dogs loved it, plus it was really good exercise for them. This is where I built Major's chest muscles up. He must have charged up and down that hill thousands of times. It was now about 5.40am, only twenty minutes to clocking off. I said to Bob, "One last throw and I'm off back to Bower."

Sod's law as always, Bob's last throw was huge and his dog, Ace, lost sight of it. The ball was lost. Bob was now trying to redirect his dog to search for the lost ball in the grass. As I left, making my way back to Bower, we were the only two dogs on in Bristol that night and I wouldn't go home until he showed up.

I had been back at Bower a good twenty minutes and there was still no sign of Bob. This turned into thirty minutes, and still no Bob. I was in the tack room having an early cuppa with the early turn mounted man when I heard a van pull into the yard. For a few minutes we heard nothing, and then we heard some moans and groans and the sound of someone shuffling along outside the tack room.

Very slowly, the tack room door opened and Bob stumbled in. He looked like he had been in a nuclear explosion. His clothes were ripped, his trousers torn, the sleeve of his coat was hanging off and his shirt was ragged. He had numerous nicks and cuts to his face and forehead, his hands were cut and bleeding, his skin had been torn off his palms and shins, his eyes were black and his nose was bleeding – he was in a dreadful state. He reminded me of those old *Laurel & Hardy* films where poor old Stan Laurel used to get blown up and always ended up in a terrible state with a blackened face. He honestly looked like he had gone fifteen rounds with Mike Tyson and a grizzly bear, and lost!

Dinsey then elaborated on the circumstances surrounding his injuries. Apparently as I left, Bob continued to try and redirect his dog, Ace, to where the ball had landed. This was probably a good fifty yards in front of where Ace was currently searching. These heavy balls on a rope were about a fiver, and Bob was certainly not going to lose this ball if he could help it. In utter frustration at the dog not finding the ball, Bob thought, Bollocks, I'll have to go and find it myself. He said that as he started to walk down the slope, he slipped and began to lose control. He was now running down the hill quicker and quicker. His legs were going up and down frantically like pistons and he was accelerating and approaching Mach 2. His arms were going like windmills in an attempt to keep his balance. He had to make a decision; he had a dilemma. In a nanosecond, this was *Dinsey's dilemma*:

1. Do I slump on my ass now and ride out the slope to the bottom and look a prat?
2. Do I try and outrun the hill to regain control?

He chose number 2, and it was the wrong choice.

He said that as he continued to accelerate, his legs simply could not go fast enough. A crash landing was inevitable. Unfortunately, he crash-landed head first, right at that part of the slope that has the wide black tarmac footpath running through it. All of Bob's soft human bits came into bone-crunching friction with Mr Tarmac. It was not nice. Bob said the pain was excruciating. He slid, tumbled and grated his body along the path, eventually stopping by a bench.

He woke up to find the dog licking his face. Then he had to climb the hill, drive back to Bower and tell this sad tale.

To anyone interested, that ball on a rope, worth a fiver, is still in the grass somewhere at the base of Brandon's Hill.

Ticker's in the Pink

This is a quick little story that I thought was quite funny. This happened prior to my joining the dogs in 1978.

One particular handler by the nickname of Ticker was a bit of a Del Boy, wheeler-dealer type of character.

One night Ticker somehow clouted the front wing of his dog van. After discussions with the group skipper it was decided that Ticker would take the van home, where he had a large, well-equipped garage. He would beat out the dents and re-spray the wing; no POLAC, no reports, no problem!

This was duly done, and the van returned to the Bower at 6am for a going off shift. No problem yet. At 9am when days came on and Brian Langley was on the prowl, Ticker's blooper came to light.

The paint gun he used to spray the dog van wing had not been thoroughly cleaned out. The previous paint job must have been on a red car, because in daylight Ticker's Ford Escort van's wing had a very delicate shade of pink about it.

How he talked his way out of it is anybody's guess.

A POLAC With a Difference
Late 1980s

This story is included in my book to give those ex-coppers out there that are reading this a chance to have a smirk and a giggle. In police parlance a POLAC is a road traffic accident involving a police vehicle.

We had a six-cage, purpose-built Talbot training van. This was obviously used on training days, but was also good for getting six dogs to public order offences or difficult public order football matches quickly.

Now this van was normally parked in reverse, therefore facing out midway along the fence in the Bower Ashton car park. It was always facing out because it meant a quick departure.

I was on a two-week refresher course. Brian Instone was the instructor, and Norman Stephenson from Bath was one of the other officers on the course. I think it was lunchtime, and I can briefly recall that we were somewhere we should not have been (possibly the Priddy Pasty Centre). Norman was driving the van when he hit a tree stump in the car park. This smashed the front offside headlight. Oh dear, a POLAC (police accident), but not a good place to have it. Questions would certainly be asked.

So we limped back to Bower Ashton and parked the training van front in, tight up against the side fence at the near end of the car park. This afforded us protection from prying eyes to the front offside of the Talbot.

We were just unloading the van for the day when sod's law invoked itself. Who should come out into the car park but our boss, Inspector Brian Langley? Instantly Brian smelt a rat. The Talbot was never parked face in, and never up tight to the front fence. He squeezed himself down the side of the Talbot nearest the fence and consequently discovered the smashed headlight.

He came straight out to Brian Instone and said, "What the hell has happened to the van?"

Brian Instone replied, with a deadpan face, "It's a POLAC and we're going to have it tomorrow."

Mr Langley went white! He turned around, and not even looking at Brian Instone, kept repeating, "This conversation has never taken place! This conversation has never taken place!"

Inspector Ostrich just buried his head in the sand, and we had the POLAC somewhere convenient the next day. Fundamentally, Brian Langley was a nice bloke.

Taking the Piss!

It was early December 1978. Myself and six other handlers were on a basic dog course out of Bower Ashton in Bristol. The officer in command of the course was Sgt Ron Pell. It was quite unusual to have seven dogs on a course; two of us were novice handlers, and two of the remaining five handlers were sergeants as well. There was Sgt Norman Oliver and Sgt Terry Connell. Amongst the others, two names to make you aware of are Cyril Haddy, the elder statesman, and the joker in the pack, 'Bugsy' Burton.

Due to the large number of dogs, we were using a type of Luton box van. We had a set of four double loose metal cages that went in the back. This gave us the capacity to carry eight dogs. Then we had three double seats out of some old scrap cars in the rear for us to sit on. So we actually had three people sat in the front of the lorry and five of us in the rear, with the seven dogs, plus Ron's dog Rinty, making eight dogs.

The three front seats, because of the seniority, were always Ron driving, Olly in the centre seat and the elder statesman Cyril in the front passenger seat next to the window. The rest of us were in the back, which could be accessed from the front as there was nothing blocking the front cab from the rear large space of the lorry.

Just to complete your visual image of this Winnebago luxury pad on six wheels was our mobile catering unit (MBC). Our MBC was a gas stove and kettle for making tea out in the wilds on the Mendips, and a des res built-in sink in the corner. Together with this we always carried three or four five-gallon plastic containers of water, primarily for the dogs to drink, but also for our tea.

Our shifts were mainly 9am to 4pm, and we normally took sandwiches in Mother's Pride plastic bags. Occasionally if we were up at Priddy Pool on the Mendips, we would sometimes visit the Priddy Pasty Centre of a lunchtime.

On this particular day we were going to RAF Colerne. This was an RAF/Army base, just inside Wiltshire, about twenty-five miles from Bristol along the M4 motorway. The junior leaders' regiment (boy soldiers) were based at Colerne, and it was where we could use huge hangars for quartering (searching for hidden criminals), plus the large expanses of grass between the runways were ideal for tracking and criminal work. I don't think it's a working airfield like Brize Norton, but the runways were still present and serviceable, and great for hard surface tracking.

Anyhow, we had had a good day's training, and at about 3pm we were all loaded up. Ron said, "If you want a piss have one now, because I won't be stopping on the motorway."

As we start to travel back, this brilliant con was instigated by Bugsy Burton and Terry Connell. Terry shouted up to Ron, "Sorry, Ron, but I need a piss."

Ron said, "Tough shit, I told you to go earlier."

Bugsy shouted out to Terry, "Have a piss in the sink, it only drains out under the lorry."

Ron went spare: "Don't you dare, you dirty bastard, we wash our tea cups in that sink!"

So Terry duly had a pee in his Mother's Pride plastic bag. He explained to Cyril what he had done, and that he was very carefully going to hand Cyril the bag of piss to throw out of the window. This was done, no problem. To be politically correct Cyril should have emptied the pee out, but understandably he didn't want Terry Connell's urine all over his hands so he just slung it out onto the grass verge. Mission accomplished!

The stage was set, and now the con.

Bugsy had primed me, about ten miles on, just as we were approaching the M32. I shouted out to Ron, "Sorry, Ron, you'll have to stop, I need a piss as well."

Ron replied, "Do what Terry did – piss in a bag and give it to Cyril. Do not piss down the sink!"

I then pretended to piss into a bag. I stood in the corner of the van. Bugsy had poured some lukewarm water out of the kettle into another Mother's Pride plastic bag and handed it to me. I then made my way up the back of the van towards the rear of Cyril's head. Bear in mind he was facing forward and had not witnessed any of the shenanigans that had been going on in the back.

I was holding the bag, which I suppose had about a pint of fluid inside it. Cyril was opening the window in preparation for dispensing with the offending bag. As Cyril turned to face me with his hand held up to accept the bag, this happened. The Mother's

Pride bag was level with Cyril's forehead, and Cyril was just about to take possession of the bag when Bugsy appeared from nowhere and shouted, "Dah-dah!", and he punctured the bag twice with a Biro pen. Suddenly warm fluid poured over Cyril's face, and some actually went into his mouth. He was soaked.

Cyril went ballistic! He tried to get over the seats at me and Bugsy, but forgot that he had his seat belt on. He was shouting and spluttering, "You c***s! I'll f*****g kill you!"

The van was rocking and rolling all over the place. Ron and Cyril were both very unhappy bunnies. Everyone else in the van, however, was nearly pissing themselves with laughter. Ron steadied the van, we got off the M32 and pulled in. By jingo, we had a very irate and upset Cyril. It didn't help that everybody else, with the exception of Ron, was laughing their heads off. Bugsy did eventually convince Cyril that the fluid was in fact warm water out of the kettle.

Dick 'Bugsy' Burton passed away a few years back. He was a great dog trainer and a fantastic guy. Goodness knows what havoc he is causing St Peter now!

Muddy Waters

This non-event happened on nights at the Bath & West showground in early June 1979. The Bath & West show attracts thousands of visitors in June every year. It is a brilliant day out with a host of agricultural attractions, shows and displays.

All of the visitors are normally gone by 7pm at the latest. However, hundreds of folk are still in and around the showground overnight. All of the staff who man the stalls stay on site, a lot of them bunked down adjacent to their display caravans, protecting their valuable goods. Then there are all of the herdsmen and animal-related persons who remain on site for their cattle, sheep, pigs, horses, goats etc. Most of these people head for the Herdsman's beer tent of an evening. This can become lively, to say the least, when these farming folk have had a few sherbets.

However, this particular story centres around a decision (not mine) that was made by the senior handler accompanying me on this particular night shift. No names, no pack drill was the expression I recall.

Well, in true Jethro fashion, what happened was myself and dog handler X had been on patrol in and around the Bath & West showground all night. We were on a 7pm–7am shift out of Bower. This meant we were on site at Pilton from around 8pm through till 6am.

The night had been uneventful, most probably because it absolutely hammered down torrential rain most of the night. The showground was a quagmire of mud. It was horrible! I was only thinking about the poor visitors attending later that day. They were going to get plastered.

Around 4.30am, as it was thinking of getting light, our attentions were drawn to our two dogs. I had my first dog Dena at the time, the long-haired GSD who usually looked cute and pretty, but not today. This morning she looked knackered, covered in mud and bedraggled. My colleague's dog, who was also long-haired, was looking similar. Both dogs honestly looked dreadful, plus they had been chasing each other all night, rolling in the mud.

We had a chat and realised that if we put them in the van like this, not only would we have to wash them when we got back to Bower, but we would also have to clean the van out. This meant we would not be getting home until 9am (the rush hour traffic). Oh dear – a decision had to be made, and my colleague made it!

All of us kept old towels back at Bower in our lockers. This meant that if the dogs were washed we could dry them off at the kennels prior to putting them in the rear of our private cars for the journey home.

At the showground there were, I believe, two purpose-built permanent swimming pools. Normally adjacent to these pools you would have temporary pools. Everything would have a price tag, but the permanent pool company had obviously invested in siting a couple of small permanent pools. These two pools looked beautiful. In our torch lights they were turquoise blue and the water looked lovely, and so inviting.

Now, we only used the smaller of the two pools, but we did give both dogs a prolonged swim and brisk hand wash in the swimming pool.

After about five minutes, two things had occurred:

1. The dogs were a hell of a lot cleaner, and now both kept on a tight lead. There was no way they were going to be allowed to run off and get dirty again.
2. What had previously looked like a pool in paradise, possibly on a Greek island, now resembled Weston-super-Mare at low tide. Mud, mud, mud and more mud. The tiled surround of the pool looked horrendous. We somehow rubbed away the paw prints.

It was just getting light. We moved away quietly and a different two handlers were down at the showground that night.

MAJOR
LET THE STORIES BEGIN

Introduction

Major was an operational police dog for almost five years, from 12th December 1979 until 13th August 1984. A hundred and thirty-one criminal arrests were credited to Major at eighty-nine incidents.

A loaded Magnum revolver and numerous other items of stolen property were recovered by Major. Major bit thirty-four people: nineteen criminals, seven police officers and eight innocent members of the public. He also nipped me dozens of times.

If Major had been a boxer, his record would have been:

- Fights – ninety incidents attended.
- Wins – eighty-seven incidents with arrests.
- Draws – one Newtown incident.
- No contest – one man on a bicycle.
- Defeats – one, to police horse George.

Major was born around August 1978. I viewed him on 17th September 1979 at the home of Marie and George from Kingswood, Bristol. Major was about thirteen months old, the same age as my youngest daughter, Laura. At this time my wife Linda and I had three daughters: Janet, five, Marie, three, and Laura, one.

Over the next five years Major was to become a truly fantastic, yet ferocious, police dog. He honestly was one of a kind; the type of dog that comes along once in a generation.

I am certainly not saying he was the best operational dog that

Bristol or Avon & Somerset ever had, but he was up there in the top six in my opinion. Dick Burton's dog, Bruce (before my time), also had a formidable reputation as "one hell of a tasty dog", likewise Jimbo's Rocky.

Major was not in the class of Pete Richard's Dusky or any of Andy Lloyd's or Jeff Poole's national champion-standard dogs. However, as a street dog he was undoubtedly amazing – no frills. Like Ronseal, Major did what it said on the tin: he attacked and arrested criminals. If it meant he had to track to attack he would, if he had to search to attack he would. He really was a biting machine.

Major Off Duty: a Family's Perspective

Marie Henderson, née Chaplin, Pete's middle daughter

One of my favourite childhood memories was playing with Major in the back garden, watching my sister Laura riding on his back while I ran alongside of them. It was an incredible feeling of such friendship. Our Major was one of a kind, and a valued member of the Chaplin family.

Janet Jones, née Chaplin, Pete's eldest daughter

When I look back at the times spent with Major, I remember him as a member of the family. Whenever myself or one of my sisters went out into the garden, Major would be jumping up and down and whimpering inside the kennel for us to let him out. He would kiss our fingers through the wire mesh as we opened the kennel door, and he would run in circles around our legs showing us that he was happy to see us, and then he would run over to the kitchen door looking for Dad.

Major was always out playing in the garden with us; he would let us chase him around our quite large back garden, and we would throw toys for him to fetch and bring back to us (although the toys didn't ever last long). Dad taught us how to give Major a biscuit and how he would hand you a paw as if to say, "Please". We would tell him to "Sit" and then say, "Gently" as he carefully took his biscuit from our fingers.

Major had a particularly close bond with my youngest sister, Laura. At that time, she was the only person he would allow to take toys or bones out of his mouth.

He was such a clever dog, and I believe he understood that Laura was the baby of the family, and that with her he had to be extra gentle. Whilst we girls played in the garden Major would sometimes lie down quietly and watch us. When it got too hot he would lie in the shade by the kitchen door and keep an eye on us just like any older member of the family.

As I was four and six years older than Marie and Laura, I can recall Major being almost 'human-like', if it hadn't had been for his four legs and furry coat.

I can remember that when Dad was going to work and he stepped up to the kennel in uniform, Major would change and become very businesslike and raring to go. But then at the end of the shift he would come home and once again become the gentlest playful friend you could wish for.

Laura Holderness, née Chaplin, Pete's youngest daughter
Everybody has that one special friend that they remember from their childhood. The one who knew you inside out and always managed to make you smile. For me that special friend just happened to have 4 legs. Major was my first friend and my best friend and although I was only little when he had to go I can remember a piece of me felt missing. He was my dad's boy but above all I remember a gorgeous fun-loving dog with whom I shared a bond I'll never forget.

Linda Chaplin, Pete's wife
I knew that Pete wanted to be a dog handler very soon after we had met in August 1974. We were married in 1975 and he went on dogs three years later in 1978.

He was on dogs for twenty years, and we had lots of different dogs in that time. The two that were always my favourites were Major and his last dog, Jason.

We did have a lady dog called Dena who was lovely for the first year, but I don't think she was up to the job, and she went to be a pet with John Claridge (who was on the motorbikes).

Major really was a wonderful dog. At home he was never any trouble. He loved the children and he got on really well with Pete's mum and dad, who spoiled him terribly. He had a special bond with our youngest daughter, Laura; they were about the same age, and they seemed inseparable.

Yes, there were the two times when Major reacted aggressively when he thought that the children were under threat, but apart from those he was fantastic.

I will tell you about Jason in Book 2.

One amazing feature of Major was that, despite all of his aggression and eagerness to attack and bite things, at home, to a large degree, he was a pussycat. There were, however, one or two exceptions.

I met Linda on 17th of August 1974. We got engaged on 1st of April 1975 and married on the 1st of November 1975. Now have four children and eight grandchildren.

Linda knew from the moment we met that I wanted to be a dog handler. She was 100% supportive in my quest to join the dog section.

In my twenty years she was never that close to any of my dogs, with the exception of Major, and at the end, Jason.

The dogs always lived in the kennel at the bottom of the garden; however, when off-duty and if we were at home they were invariably loose in the garden.

Major would lie on the patio next to the back door. If he was lucky he poked his head into the kitchen once every six months.

My mum and dad lived about three streets away and they spoiled Major rotten, always saving the cuts of meat off the Sunday joint or buying him dog chews and the like. Despite all of his aggression, Major loved them to bits and on more than one occasion we would realise he was missing and then we'd get a phone call from Mum saying, "Your dog's here if you want him!"

They were all working dogs and not pets, but the bond I had

with all of them (as all handlers do) was special.

Major's attitude to my three daughters was wonderful and caring. He never displayed any aggression towards any of them. He was very protective of the two younger ones and had a particularly strong bond with Laura. Both Marie and Laura would try to sit on his back; they would play rough and tumble with him all day and there were never any problems. Janet, my eldest daughter, also got on great with Major but she was a few years older and was not quite so enamoured with having a dog as her best friend. As time went on, Laura and Major became inseparable and he used to follow her around the garden all day in good weather.

All police dogs lived with their handlers and families. The dog had a large purpose-built kennel in the garden. It was not an absolute requirement; however in the late 70s, it was considered desirable that new dog handlers had a stable lifestyle and were married, preferably with children. This ensured the dog was introduced to a cross-section of society, typical to that he might encounter on the streets.

In Major's case, when off duty and at home he was predominately out of the kennel in the back garden. The kids would be playing with him most of the time or just brushing and smoothing him.

His normal place of abode when not in the kennel was lying by the kitchen door, out on the patio. He very seldom ventured in the kitchen, as Linda was not too keen on dog hairs in the house. However, once or twice a year he would lie down on the kitchen floor for ten to fifteen minutes until he felt he was about to outstay his welcome, and then he would sneak out to take up his normal place just outside the back door.

One event of the day which is loved by all dogs is feeding time. Our dogs were always fed after work, or if on a day off, at around 5pm. A bucket of fresh water was always available in their kennel.

Over the years different feeding regimes and menus were introduced, but in Major's time his meal was a large tin of Pedigree Chum and two tins full of dog biscuits. I always used to add a small amount of boiling water which mixed the meat and gravy in with the biscuits. Occasionally, I would nick an egg or two from the kitchen and some milk, as a little treat. I am sure I occasionally added cooking or olive oil to enhance his coat.

Now, here is an interesting fact: I usually fed Major in his kennel. He was always eager to get to his grub, quite often barking loudly as if to say, "Hurry up." If I put his food down and walked away, no problem. However, if I stayed in the kennel or even just outside, after a few seconds with his head in the feeding bowl he would curl his lip to show his teeth and growl (basically saying, "Piss off and leave me alone"). The unbelievable exception to this would be Laura. Not that I actively encouraged this, but Laura could walk into Major's kennel whilst he was feeding. She would pick up his feeding bowl and walk off around the garden with it. He would follow, his ears flat to his head in submission, and then he would continue feeding when she put his bowl down. This could go on for three or four times before he would gently nudge her out of the way in order to finish his food.

Major at Home: Incident 1

I had had Major about six months, so this was around March 1980. I was just returning home after a day shift; it was about 4.30pm and the light was beginning to fade. It was a dull, bleak mid-March day, quite cold in fact. Our house is on a bend, and as I pulled up in my horrible turquoise Hillman Hunter Estate I could see my wife Linda standing at the front gate holding my youngest daughter Laura, who was about eighteen months old and was toddling.

Major, in the rear of the estate car, caught sight of Laura and began to whimper excitedly. Laura and Major were best mates, and both were excited to be seeing each other. As I slowed down to pull up just below our front gate, my attention was drawn to two teenage girls who were walking up the road. One of the girls was wearing a thick woollen (what I called wigwam) coat which resembled a big, heavy cape-like garment; it had no sleeves but had slits where pockets should have been, and the wearer could either keep their hands warm inside the garment or push their hands and arms out through the slits. I purposely delayed exiting the car until I was happy and confident that these two teenagers had passed our gate and were safely out of the way.

They had traversed our gate, passing Linda and Laura, and I was confident on letting Major out of the car. Then in slow motion, but also so very quickly, this happened: Linda put Laura down and she started to toddle down the fifteen yards to greet me and Major; then Linda turned to go back indoors. I got out of the car and was just in the process of opening the car's tailgate when Laura tripped on a raised paving slab, fell over and started crying. The girl in the wigwam coat turned around, ran back and was bending down to pick Laura up. Major saw all of this, and as I opened the tailgate slightly he hit it with his head. The tailgate flew up and hit me under the chin, knocking me over. Major, growling like the Hound of the Baskervilles, leapt out of the car and attacked the teenage girl, who in his mind was hurting Laura and making her cry. He had her pinned to the ground and was growling aggressively. Getting to my feet, I managed to get him to release as quickly as I could.

The coat had absorbed quite a bit of the attack, and although she went to the hospital, her injuries were not as serious as they otherwise could have been. She was a local girl, and I knew her parents. I later went to apologise for the incident with some flowers; however, her mum, who thank goodness was very pro-police, said, "Your dog was doing what he is trained to do and looking after his family."

The attitude of the family towards me and my job was typical of the 'live and let live' mentality that existed between me and the local community. Lockleaze is an estate of working-class people who work hard and play hard. I was a council-house boy on a council estate who represented the law. But I never brought the job home, and consequently I never had any difficulties with neighbours and locals who may not have been so observant of authority as others.

To say that Major was protective of Laura was an understatement. He really did keep any an eye on her, just like a big brother.

Major at Home: Incident 2
Could Not Do It Again Even if He Tried

I think this funny little incident occurred around the summer of 1982. Linda ran a Littlewoods mail order business, with friends and family ordering from the catalogue. I believe the couriers who used to deliver the goods were White Arrow.

On this sunny afternoon I was unfortunately cleaning the front bedroom windows, and I was half-hanging out the box room window with my bottle of Windolene and a duster. As always, these things happen so quickly, and I was engrossed in my task, knowing very well that Linda would be checking the corners for smears on the window. I hardly noticed the White Arrow van pull up outside my house. He was in the normal Dormobile-type van with a sliding door. The first I truly realised that we had a caller was when I heard the front gate squeak into life. Our front gate was very noisy; it had never been oiled but was like our early warning system because you could hear the loud squeak long before anyone rang our front doorbell. It also had an incredibly tough and resilient spring on it. This meant it was quite hard to open, and if you let it close by itself then the clang of metal on metal was significant. The purpose of the heavy spring was to keep Major in. As most dogs' eye level is only at about 2'6", an average height garden gate is adequate to contain most dogs.

On this sunny day all of our three girls were in the back garden playing with Major. I heard the squeak of the gate, then the clang of the metal as the heavy spring automatically closed the gate. Then very briefly as I looked up I heard this 'happy chappie' courier whistling some tune. He was an oldish chap and he was carrying two quite large cardboard boxes. He had left the engine running and the sliding door open.

He had taken about five or six steps towards the front door when a sound echoed from within the bowels of our back garden – Major had heard the gate open. There was a blood-curdling growl and gut-wrenching gnashing of teeth emanating from just around the corner of the house. Suddenly you could hear barking and panting getting closer and closer. You could hear the sound of huge pads pounding along the pathway that runs along the side of our house. Then it appeared: the hound from hell, his claws slipping and sliding as he took the corner at what seemed to be 70mph. The poor courier – the blood drained from his face and the boxes went flying. Despite his age he made the gate in a time that Linford Christie would have been proud of. Major, whose eyes had now turned green, was closing in and he wanted blood. To my utter amazement the courier leapt the gate in the sitting position, straight into the driver's seat of the Dormobile. He was in gear and moving just as Major ploughed into the front gate. What a lucky bunny this chap was. He could never do that again no matter how hard he might try. Fear is a funny thing – it can make you do superhuman things.

After this the White Arrow man used to rattle our gate and quickly sit back in his van for thirty seconds before he dared enter Major's territory.

At this point I think it may be useful for me to explain a few things about Major that will help you understand the beast a little better.

1. He was not a huge dog, but not small. He weighed about 90–95lbs, but was like a little bull.
2. To develop his muscles (chest and front, plus hind legs) I used to go to the top of Brandon Hill and throw his ball down the steep slope. He was mad on retrieving and it was the countless runs back up that steep hill that over the months and years developed his physique.
3. Bearing in mind that I was the A Division dog handler on our group, I visited Brandon Hill nearly every shift. As stated, his desire to retrieve was unquenchable – he would retrieve until he dropped.
4. The other thing he loved was biting, chewing and carrying heavy objects around in his mouth. I did my daily walks on Purdown around the old gun emplacements by the BT Tower,

where there were plenty of bricks for him to pick up and carry. His party trick was carrying two bricks cemented together. Also, he would bite and carry metal. Lots of dogs would shy away from carrying metal; however, Major loved it. No problem whatsoever.

5. Because of all of his biting and chewing of various objects (he once destroyed a skittle ball down at the St Annes Board Mills), his canine teeth in particular became somewhat shorter/blunter, and consequently if he bit someone that individual was not left with neat little puncture wounds.

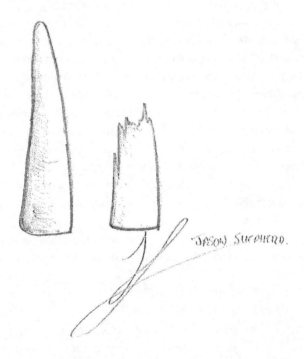

6. Also, some dogs may have had a greater pounds-per-square-inch pressure to their bite than Major, perhaps a bigger GSD or Rottweiler. However, Major had that additional natural instinct that caused him to shake violently anything that he bit.

Major's Funny Ways

Major was first and foremost a living piece of police equipment, and he had the potential to be ferocious and intimidating.

The trick was never to look directly at him, and certainly not to stare at him. He was not a pet so it was not a good idea to approach him and attempt to pet him or smooth him.

Ironically, at home he was a complete pussycat, and at no point displayed any aggression towards any of our family. In fact, Laura used to ride on his back and Marie would follow him around the garden holding onto his tail.

My parents were daily visitors to our home (they only lived three streets away from us) and Major loved them to bits. My mum in particular was always buying him little doggie treats and the like. I think that I have already mentioned that on a number of occasions, I have received telephone calls from my mum saying, "Have you lost something?" Lo and behold, Major would have somehow escaped the garden and run around to my mum's for a bit of spoiling.

On our daily walks on Purdown he would love to pick up and carry bricks, sticks and metal of all sorts – with him, the heavier the object, the more he seemed to enjoy struggling to carry it.

His desire to chase and retrieve any object was astonishing. He would continue until my arm was aching and I could throw no more.

He was one of a kind whose reputation on the streets amongst the coppers we worked with was fantastic. He was a legend.

Working as a Team – Our Office

For me and Major our office was our Ford Escort van. Major always occupied the left-hand cage that was behind the front passenger seat. This was because there was a sliding door on the front of the cage which enabled Major to be loose with me in the front cab if necessary.

Experience taught me many things. One important thing I learned was not to assume that your dog has seen what you have seen. Out on the street the dog's eye level is about 2'6", whereas ours is about 5'6" high. That's why in the van I found it advantageous at times to have Major up front with me, tuned in to events. Many a time Major exited via the van's front windows, saving vital seconds.

Fights Lost

At the introduction I compared Major to a boxer and explained how he had ninety fights and won all but three. Here are the details of the three he didn't win.

The Draw

This was around November 1981 at New Town Hassell Drive, St Judes. A very big man (no previous convictions) discovered that his wife was having an affair whilst he was on nights. He returned home to find his wife in bed with another man. He went berserk and then beat this guy to a pulp. Unfortunately, he then also beat up the two officers who were called to the initial assault. This guy was the size of Goliath. He stood out in the road defying the police and inviting officers to join him in combat and ultimately defeat.

I was summoned to the incident, and in typical fashion I parked up around the corner from all the nonsense. As I ran around the corner with Major on his lead to confront this maniac, I unfortunately came too close to a very nice chap who was just getting out of his car with a tasty takeaway that was intended for his supper. With the strike speed of a king cobra, Major gave him a flying bite on his thigh as a sort of precursor to the main event with Goliath. Another innocent victim bitten (sorry).

Now the criminal was a big bloke, who was taking on all comers and winning. Probably today he would have been tasered with 50 million volts. Anyway, there we were like two old gunslingers at the OK Corral at Dodge City. Goliath stood defiant in the middle of the road shouting obscenities. I had Major up on his hind legs, his eyes had gone green and he was spitting fire. I challenged Goliath, identifying myself and ordering him to surrender himself to the nearby officers. He told me to f*** off! I sent Major for the first time. Major attacked him full-on, latching onto one of his thighs, which were the size of tree trunks. This guy put his hands onto Major's snout and twisted his whole nose and upper jaw. I heard a nasty sound of *schwarzzz* (dog flesh and cartilage being crushed). His hands were huge, and he threw Major across the road like a rag doll.

Major got up, shook himself off and then *wham!* It was the second attack. He was back in with another four puncture wounds. Again, *schwarzzz* – Goliath bent Major's nose and tossed him away. Now this was really pissing Major off. For the third and final time *wham!* Another four puncture wounds. That's twelve puncture wounds in all.

At this point Goliath shouted, "OK! I give in, get this f****r off me."

Goliath was charged with numerous assaults and injuries. He refused all medical treatment. When asked if he wanted to complain about his injuries he simply replied with, "No." That's why I put this contest down as a draw.

The No Contest

It was nights and I was doubled up with Sgt Vernon Essex. Vernon's dog was injured and could not work. He was basically my driver. This was around April 1983. The location was His Majesty's Cinema in Stapleton Road, Easton. A burglary had occurred and the offender was making off down the lane at the rear of the cinema. PC Mike Povey was still guarding the unsecured front door. The lane ran along the side of the cinema, basically parallel with the M32.

Vernon took the main entrance by Mike Povey and I went to the far end of the lane near to Stapleton Road Railway Station. As I entered the lane with Major, to my surprise I saw the villain, but he was cycling towards me on a bicycle. This burglar on the bike had his arms full of goodies from the cinema shop. Upon seeing me, he nearly fell off his bike. He dropped all the sweets and chocolates that he had nicked, he stopped abruptly, turned around and cycled off away from me back down the lane. Major was only too willing to give chase, which he did. Unfortunately, he had never trained for a fleeing criminal riding a bike. Major not only caught up with the cycling burglar, he overtook him, still, in his mind, looking for a villain. Then *kapow!* Major found what he thought was a legitimate target, namely Constable Michael Povey (who was still guarding the unsecured cinema door). PC Povey got bitten and went to hospital.

The villain, laughing his socks off, cycled past Mike getting chewed up by Major and was lost to sight. Although we had the last laugh – it was half an hour later when the cyclist was nicked in Fishponds. Result – no contest!

Major's One and Only Defeat
Sunday Morning Day Tour (9am–4pm), 1980, Bower Ashton

In the paddock at Bower there was a large brown police horse. Major went into the large paddock, cocked his leg and had a pee. He then went up to the horse, sniffed the horse, and the horse sniffed him. There was no reaction and no problems. We then went out on patrol.

At about 3.45pm, just prior to going home, a big brown police horse was still in the paddock. I put Major into the paddock for one final pee before going home and discovered that they had swapped horses. This was a big mistake, as this big brown police horse was George, the legendary dog hater. Major sniffed the horse and *kapow!* The horse double-barrelled with both hind legs and Major flew thirty feet through the air. His jaw was not only broken, but where the jaws were out of alignment they were stuck together. Major chased George all around the paddock, but he couldn't bite him because his jaws were locked. Surgery for Major followed, and a vet bill too large to think about. Result – defeat!

I will now relate some of the amazing stories that Major and I became involved with. In an attempt to clarify and confirm some of these incidents, I made a number of appeals through various NARPO (National Association of Retired Police Officers) websites. The response was amazing, and some stories will be followed by anecdotal comments from former Avon & Somerset Police officers who either witnessed various events or in fact were actual victims themselves. I have already partly quoted Dave Hutchins of Trinity Road fame, who said of Major, "I had seen Major in action many times, and the beast had no mercy for friend or foe."

Basic Course with Jake, 1984

Avon and Somerset Dog Section, 50th Anniversary Reunion, 2007

In garden with Major, 1979

Major at three months old, 1978

Marie and Major in garden, 1980

Marie, Laura and Major

On patio with Defer and Adam (two months old), 1988

Dog kennel in the garden

Parade at Central Police Station, 1970s

Trinity Road nick (rear yard), 1970s

Major, School Liaison at Clifton College, 1970s

Major, Dog of the Year, 1981

With Dena on initial dog course, 1978

Police District Training School at Chantmarle, Dorset

Major in Victoria Park, 1983

Major in the garden holding paw up in a display of non-aggression, 1984

Charactature of Peter and Major, courtesey of Rob Staplin, 2009

MAJOR'S ARRESTS BEGIN

In all of the following stories, I will not be identifying the names or details of those persons arrested. By ensuring the prisoners remaining nameless I am protecting their right to anonymity and me from possible slander or prosecution.

Because I wanted to include all of Major's 131 criminal arrests I hope that you will appreciate that sometimes the details are brief and factual, My diary triggers my memory for some of the more memorable jobs, but for some of the mundane day-to-day prisoners I honestly remember very little. Bear in mind it's over thirty years ago.

All of these details are taken from my dogs section diary that I kept for my twenty years on dogs.

11th November 1979
Location: Burglary at a Warehouse in Hotwells
Three burglars detained on premises by dog. One traffic officer was very nearly bitten. (The traffic guys came into the area too soon after the arrest. Policeman sometimes foolishly assume, "I am a policeman, a police dog won't bite me!")

13th December 1979
The Lodge Causeway Knifeman – Bristol D Division
This incident occurred on a late turn in mid-December 1979. This was in the Fishponds area of Bristol. Two teenagers were in Lodge Causeway when they were approached by a vagrant-type man, in his early twenties, wearing a very long, tatty overcoat. He originally asked

these kids for a cigarette and then asked for money. An argument and a struggle ensued, and both teenagers were threatened with a knife.

The offender ran off and was seen to enter the side door of an old café in Lodge Causeway, which at this time was being used as a 'doss house' for individuals who were homeless and on benefits.

I had to make my way from the city centre in heavy traffic. It was about 7.30pm and the fast run from town to Fishponds with the twos and blues on had certainly got mine and Major's adrenaline going.

Upon arriving at the scene, I left Major in the van whilst I had a brief chat with the local officers who filled me in on details and gave a description of the offender. Upon getting Major out of the van I immediately noticed how his demeanour was totally different to that of my previous dog, Dena. Dena, on the van's doors being opened, would have gracefully jumped down and remained very close to me, looking up at me constantly for reassurance.

Major's exit was somewhat like an Exocet missile. Firstly, I had to lasso his neck into the chain on his lead. This was no mean feat as he was trying to get out of the cage ASAP. He flew out of the van, causing the police officers in attendance to take a few swift steps backwards, allowing Major sufficient space for his requirements. He then began barking quite aggressively at everyone and anyone. We were led into the café and told that our suspect was in a first-floor bedsit. Officers led us up to this bedroom door, giving us plenty of breathing space. I had managed to shut Major up but he was pulling very hard on his chain and lead and his panting sounded horrendous.

I did not even try the door handle, but yelled, "Police! I have a dog – don't move." I kicked the flimsy bedroom door open. Major was now barking, and the other officers were quite a few paces behind me (which was very wise). Upon entering the room, I saw a single bed up against the wall. It was covered in a candlewick bedspread, just like we had at home in Hemmings Parade in the early 1950s. Something was obviously underneath this covering, lying in the bed. I approached the bed, and with a sudden yank I pulled this bedspread off the bed. This immediately exposed the young vagrant offender, who was fully clothed with overcoat and boots. He was holding a small knife. Major, who was stood at my side, was given a quick tap on his side with my knee (In his early days this was to become his 'on' switch), and he went bananas. His front legs were up on the bed and he was spitting fire at this guy. The offender threw the knife down and the other officers were called in to take him into custody.

Diary comment was: *Major very effective.*

Major's Turn-On Switch

Nudging Major's right shoulder with the outside of my left knee was the signal. As they said in *Gladiator*, "On my signal, release hell", and my goodness me, it worked, although I didn't have to use it very often because Major as a rule was always switched on. The comment that I wrote in my diary after this event was: *Major – very effective.*

13th January 1980
Dundry Driver Goes AWOL
Location: The Hills Around the Top of Dundry to the South of Bristol
(J Division Just Inside the Weston-super-Mare District)

At around midnight on 13th January 1980 I was called to R/V with a Nailsea police unit in the vicinity of Dundry Lane with Ham Lane at the top of Dundry. A stolen car had been pursued from the Long Ashton, Barrow Gurney area; it had been lost for a few minutes at the top of Dundry and then suddenly abandoned at the dead end of Ham Lane. The driver's door was open and it had obviously been hotwired. Thankfully the pursuing unit from Nailsea had remained in their police car and had not contaminated the crime scene. This meant that the only human scent leading from that vehicle had to be the offender. Unfortunately, too many overzealous coppers in their size 12 boots trample over most crime scenes and then blatantly deny that they have walked anywhere.

On this occasion, I took Major out of the van and put on his tracking harness. When using tracking harnesses, a number of things are achieved:

1. A degree of control. The harness fits around the body and has a metal loop at the centre of the dog's back, to which you clasp your thirty-foot track line.
2. That thirty-foot line gives you flexibility if the dog is wavering on and off track due to wind, weather, terrain or whatever.
3. The harness acts as an automatic trigger that instantly tells the dogs, "We are going tracking – put your nose to the ground, search for a scent/ground disturbance and follow the track."

As soon as the harness was on, Major went into action. I know that in the back of his mind he was thinking, If I can find a track and follow it, then there is a good chance I can find them and bite them.

He snorted and sniffed all around the car for a minute or so and then *bang!* We were off! He located a track which went off to the right immediately, over a five-bar gate and straight across a field heading in the general direction of Withywood. Then at the bottom of this field we went over another gate and into another field, straight across this one and then we skirted around to the right, following the hedgerow. When tracking across open ground at night I never used my torch (you don't want to warn the bad guys that you're coming) and always had my radio on very low (to keep sound to a minimum). As far as I can recall we then went into another large field, and once again we skirted the edge. The last thing you want to encounter is cows. Cows are inquisitive; they come towards you, plus they knacker up the track. From this field, we crossed a road into another field, and then a small copse and then into Steep Lane.

I imagine I had been tracking for about fifteen minutes and covered about six hundred yards when suddenly Major started barking and tried to burrow into the thick hedge on my right. I shone my torch, and to my delight I made out a pair of trainers with feet and legs, hiding in the bush. This villain tried to play dumb; however, Major was getting more and more wound up.

I stopped Major making physical contact and yelled, "You are asking to get bitten, my old son! Stop being a bloody idiot and come out slowly." A twenty-one-year-old local man was arrested and charged; a guilty plea followed and a few other outstanding jobs cleared up.

Diary comment: *Good job, dog.*

25th January 1980

Next job was a nice little job and nothing spectacular. After a spate of burglaries in the Broadmead shopping area, Major located two burglars hiding on the roof of WH Smith.

4th April 1980
Location: Arnside, Southmead Estate, C Division

This was a smash-and-grab at a local fruit and veg shop. A short search found the offender hiding amongst refuse bins at the rear of the shops.

5th May 1980
Location: Weston-super-Mare, J Division

This was a very basic Section 5 public order arrest on, I believe, a May Bank Holiday Sunday. Weston-super-Mare on the North Somerset coast was, and is, a seaside town that attracts huge volumes of visitors, especially on bank holidays in the spring and summer.

In the early 1980s the skinhead 'yob' culture was alive and thriving, and even in a small place like Weston-super-Mare, the local skinheads were a nuisance. The bank holiday was the perfect catalyst for confrontation between locals and the various gangs of Bristol skinheads who eagerly made the thirty-minute train journey down to Weston from Bristol Temple Meads.

Those lovely Weston skins were very considerate, and in order to help us identify them they very kindly had a spider's web tattoo inked on their necks. This little gang affiliation tattoo helped us immensely when it came to segregating Weston skins from Bristol skins.

We had been on the seafront since about 11am, and the crowds were steadily building up. On this Sunday there were three double-crewed dog vans patrolling the resort. This meant we had a total of six police dogs available to respond to any outbreaks of disorder.

In addition to the dogs there were also four of our equine friends or "hay burners" (police horses) patrolling the seafront. We worked very closely with our mounted colleagues and it was great to know that they were available if the need arose.

Silly little running skirmishes had been occurring, mostly instigated by the Weston skins; however, they were quite clever, and although on the loud side and obnoxious, the gang of about ten yobbos knew not to cross the line.

One particular yobbo was wearing a plastic police helmet, carrying a plastic toy truncheon and constantly blowing a whistle. He was taking the piss big time, but not quite enough to warrant being arrested.

For over an hour he and his gang were taunting us up and down Regent Street. This is the main road which leads from the centre of town down onto the seafront and Grand Pier. This is where lots of amusement arcades are situated, and these arcades, full of lesser yobs, were the audience that Matey Boy and his gang of Weston skins were playing to.

After putting up with these taunts for about an hour the following incident occurred that gave me the opportunity to arrest Matey Boy for a public order offence. As I said, little confrontations had been occurring for about an hour or so, but due to the heavy police presence nothing had escalated into violence.

Now around 2.30pm Matey Boy had bought himself a bag of Weston's finest potato chips, no doubt sprinkled liberally with salt and vinegar. He was stood about twenty yards in front of my dog van enjoying the culinary delight. What happened next occurred very quickly. As Matey ate his chips, a group of three or four men passed him very closely, and from nowhere a fist appeared and smacked him right in the face. The perpetrator was 'who knows who' in a mass of passing people.

Matey, his nose bleeding and plastic police helmet missing, went mad. He was cursing and swearing and suddenly threw his bag of chips straight onto the windscreen of a slow-moving holidaymaker's car, which was travelling up Regent Street towards the pier. This caused the driver to brake violently, frightening his wife and kids to death. No accident occurred, but the vehicles behind him had to take evasive action to avoid a collision. The car's windscreen was a bit of a mess, covered in mashed-up potato chips.

Here was my chance, and I was out of my van like a shot. I was joined by other nearby officers who had witnessed Matey's behaviour, and he was quickly restrained and a task force van was soon on the scene to convey Matey in custody to Weston-super-Mare Police Station.

The following morning Matey Boy was remanded in custody for three weeks for a 'not guilty' trial at the local Weston-super-Mare Magistrates Court. Three weeks later I gave evidence in court, where the Magistrates convicted Matey and only sent him to a young offenders' institution for three months.

Prior to leaving the witness box the principle Magistrate thanked me very much for helping to deal with local undesirables, who in his opinion were not only giving Weston a bad name but were having a detrimental effect on holidaymakers visiting the resort.

As I said at the start, a nothing job, but one worth recounting for you. Matey Boy should have been grateful for the Magistrates Justice, and not having received 'Major's justice'.

Diary comment: *Nasty yob.*

12th May 1980
Location: Burglary in Hotwells, Bristol
Three youths detained – my memory of this job is very sketchy and I have had to rely on my diary for the basics.

14th May 1980
Location: the White Swan Public House – Bottom of Robertson Road with Stapleton Road
A man was assaulted by two men in the bar. I was first upon the scene and detained two persons identified by the victim.

14th July 1980
Location: Embleton Road School, Southmead, Bristol

This was around 3am on the morning of 14th July 1980. The original call came in regarding a suspicious youth who was syphoning petrol from cars at various streets in and around the Southmead council estate. A little later a call came in from an early morning milkman who, whilst on his rounds, had had a car collide with his milk float and the driver of that car had run off in the vicinity of Embleton Road Junior School. Unfortunately, I was quite some distance away and by the time I got to the scene, lots of police officers were in the school grounds searching every conceivable nook and cranny. It was shortly confirmed that the car that had hit the milk float and been abandoned was in fact a stolen vehicle from Wiltshire.

The skipper in charge of the C Division lads basically said, "We've searched the school grounds and if he ever did come into the grounds, he ran straight through and he is long gone."

I was not content with this, and if you recall I said that a couple of things you need to be a good handler are patience and perseverance. I found the milkman and he indicated to me where he had last seen the offender. This was only about eighty yards from the side fence of Embleton Road School. I got Major out of the van and quickly set about fitting his tracking harness. As soon as this was attached, Major went into automatic mode with his nose close to the ground, trying to locate a track. To be honest, it was not easy bearing in mind it was most probably forty-five minutes to nearly an hour since the collision and the youth running off; the time was getting on and the track was getting older by the minute.

Major continued sniffing and snorting, and then all at once he located something and was off. The surface was a mixture of grass verge and pavement; on the grass bits he was quite positive, but going from grass to pavement, things slowed down. This was because hard surface tracking is very difficult; bearing in mind the track scent is a combination of human smell, footwear and principally ground disturbance smell. On grass and soil there is the capability for the soil or grass to be crushed and compressed by the weight of a footprint, which releases the odours of tiny organisms within the soil. However, the only disturbance possible on a hard surface like a paving slab is the tiny amount of disturbance to the thin layer of micro dust that is present on the slab's surface. It's very difficult, believe me! However, he did track, and straight up to the school perimeter fence. On the other side of the fence was a flower bed, and can you imagine my delight when, upon shining my torch onto the flower bed, I saw the distinct imprints of two shoes! Without a doubt someone had climbed that fence and then jumped from the top, landing heavily in the flower bed.

There were still one or two coppers in the area, and over the radio I informed C Division control that I had positively tracked into the school grounds and that I intended searching the school grounds myself. By now I was over the fence and in the grounds, and the few coppers that were still about had been positioned at strategic points around the outside perimeter of the school. No one but Major and I were in the grounds. At this point I intended letting the beast loose, so once again I confirmed over the air that no friendlies were within the school grounds, and consequently I did not run the risk of any coppers getting bitten. I then let Major loose with the well-proven and trusted command of, "Where is he?" Upon gaining his freedom, Major zoomed off at a fair speed of knots, whining and whimpering with anticipation as he disappeared out of sight around the first corner.

The school was a rather large, sprawling, single-storey group of attached buildings. On top of various roofs were the occasional small brick structures, which I assume stored water tanks and the like, and there were also quite a lot of aluminium air ducts spread across the roofs. I literally just wandered around, with Major coming into sight and then disappearing around yet another corner or building. When I did catch sight of him I would top up his enthusiasm with yet another, "Go on, where is he then?"

As we progressed around the various building perimeters I was beginning to become somewhat disheartened. Was that skipper right in his assumption that this tea leaf had climbed into the grounds and simply run through and out the other side, then disappeared in the maze that is Southmead council estate?

I continued on my quest, covering yet more of the school premises, still hoping that my luck might be in. Left turn, right turn, left turn, and then suddenly I found that I had turned a corner that led me down a dead end. There were single-storey school buildings to my left and to my right, and in fact up ahead of me as well. I was in a cul-de-sac of classrooms. However, my attention was drawn to Major, who was down on my right-hand side about thirty yards away. He would not leave a particular windowsill that formed part of a classroom window. His head was held high, he was snorting the air and he kept putting his front legs up on the wall just under the window ledge. Strangely enough he was not barking (this would have been the classic indication of the presence of human scent); however, he was whining and whimpering and would not leave that patch of wall. Upon joining him he became increasingly excited and did in fact bark once or twice. As I reached the window I could not believe my eyes: there on the windowsill, still just visible but fading fast, was the footprint of a boot or training shoe. I was honestly over the moon; I could not believe it. Without doubt someone had very recently climbed up via that windowsill and onto the roof.

Putting Major on his lead and securing him to a fence, I then called in the cops who had been outside. With the help of a couple of officers I managed to climb up onto the roof. All that was there was an aluminium air duct, about two feet square. This aluminium vent was just like you've seen in the Hollywood blockbuster films, like *Die Hard* with Bruce Willis. As I approached this vent system I could see that the entrance to it was off to my right; on turning and positioning myself at the entrance my heart raced as I saw that the mesh cover had been removed and was laid on the flat roof. My delight was overwhelming because upon looking into the vent and shining my torch I saw a pair of trainers containing feet, then legs, then the whole body of the car thief who had run away after colliding with the milk float. This individual was in fact an absconder from Guys Marsh Borstal, I believe in Wiltshire. He was arrested without further ado, not bitten and not injured. He did express to me that he thought he had got away with it and would have remained in situ until dawn and then quietly made his way off. A very good dog job. This villain would have evaded capture had it not been for Major.

My diary read: *Very good dog job.*

8th August 1980

Theft of a bicycle in Broadmead. One man arrested and cycle recovered.

10th August 1980
A Division Central

This was a typical silly criminal damage job. A group of youths who had had too much to drink started behaving stupidly. One in particular was extremely stupid and rolled a large empty beer barrel down Colston Street (which is a steep hill), where it crashed into a stationary unattended car, causing lots of damage. One youth arrested on description, admitted offence readily and was not bitten.

23rd August 1980
Failand
J Division

There was a burglary at a bungalow in Failand on the outskirts of Bristol. I can recall that an elderly gentleman who had been out on a summer's evening returned to find an intruder in his home. A window had been forced at the rear of the bungalow and entry gained; the intruder had made off via the broken window and disappeared from sight in the adjoining gardens.

Failand is a rural, upmarket location about five or six miles south of Bristol. In this case the control room was at Weston-super-Mare, or it may even have been controlled from Taunton. Geographically there were only three roads which basically encompassed Failand. They put roadblocks on all the relevant junctions and in effect the whole of Failand was sealed off. Although I had to travel from A Division central to the crime scene I was there in about twenty or twenty-five minutes. Picking up a track was not possible because on learning of the crime everybody and anybody went out into their front and rear gardens checking sheds, driveways, lanes, etc.

From where the offender had left the bungalow, a couple of well-meaning PC Plods had totally destroyed the scene by searching and walking everywhere, knackering any positive track.

What I decided to do was to carry out a slow and methodical search of all the gardens in the general direction of where this guy had last been seen. The description I had was of a middle-aged man, forty-five to fifty years old, quite small, about 5'6", and quite dishevelled; he looked like he had been living rough.

The difficulty I had was that I couldn't really just let Major loose because I knew too well that if left to his own devices on an open quarter he would in all probability bite anyone or anything he came across. What I decided to do was clip his chain collar onto my thirty-foot tracking line. This meant that he had the freedom to search, but I had the control and capability of having him anything from two up to thirty feet away from me.

So off we went. I had already confirmed that the police roadblocks were still in situ and that we still had the Failand area contained. It was quite a long, laborious job and what I do recall is that I was missing the retirement do of one of the dog section's legends, and that was Sgt Norman 'Ollie' Oliver. Anyway, on we went, garden after garden, searching sheds, greenhouses, outhouses – you name it, we searched it. Major was showing lots of interest nearly everywhere we went, mainly because after the fracas, as explained, everyone had been out in their gardens searching.

I don't know how far we had gone when Major made his way through one hedgerow into yet another garden, where he stopped and started rummaging around in the hedge. The narrow, restrictive bit of vegetation was too small to conceal a man, but nonetheless Major continued to root away at the base of the hedgerow. After a good few minutes he surfaced out of the hedge and he had a yellow-handled screwdriver in his mouth. This was later confirmed to have been dropped by the offender as he attempted to make good his escape.

So on we went, garden after garden. What I loved about Major was that his enthusiasm never diminished. He didn't get fed up or bored, he just kept ploughing on regardless. If I'm honest I know that the reason he kept going was probably the thought in his mind that at the end of this there may well be someone that he could attack.

We now found ourselves in quite a long, narrow garden, and as Major progressed along its perimeter hedge, his demeanour suddenly changed. I knew his telltale signs, and believe me, he was preparing for attack mode. His hackles were bristling; his tail came up and all at once he made a beeline for the row of kidney beans which were about thirty feet ahead of him. I was trying to reel him in when suddenly I heard a scream as he first reached and then entered the bean sticks. He had found our offender lying down, concealed in amongst the kidney beans.

The burglar was in fact a career criminal who had only been released two weeks earlier after a four-year stretch in Dartmoor prison.

The tracking line worked, because although very aggressive, Major only managed a minor introductory nip before I restrained him. The criminal was genuinely appreciative, and a quick guilty plea and return to prison followed.

Diary comment: *Good dog prisoner.*

11th October 1980
Bristol City v. Newcastle United
C Division

On this Saturday PC Neil Barnes and I were double-crewed when we arrested six football supporters on the Portway. These six had earlier trapped and attacked two Bristol City fans in Winterstoke Road.

17th October 1980
Psychiatric Patient from Barrow Guerney
J Division

A missing person was found wandering in Long Ashton and returned to the hospital.

20th October 1980
A Division

This was a raid on a house in St Pauls.

The offender, an escapee from borstal, was arrested when we raided a house in Brigstocke Road. The offender was wanted for robbery.

21st October 1980
B Division

10.9 assistance call – officer in trouble. School Road, Brislington. Two brothers were arrested for assault on police.

9th November 1980
B Division

The offender was arrested for burglary at the Central Trading Estate.

25th December – Christmas Day 1980
B Division

The offender was in possession of a large sheath knife, an offensive weapon, in Bishopsworth Road at 3am on Christmas morning.

31st December 1980
E Division

A very nasty sexual assault was carried out upon a seventy-four-year-old pensioner in her home at Midsomer Norton. The offender, high on drugs, had also ransacked this lady's cottage.

Although I had to travel about twenty-five miles to attend the scene, Major located the still-high offender hiding in the garden.

Guilty plea – the offender received two years' imprisonment.

Diary comment: *A nasty, evil young man.*

24th March 1981

Stop check – the offender wanted on warrant in Hotwells Road.

18th April 1981
Location – Bannerman Road School at Hallows Road, Easton, Bristol

I attended the school as a result of the school's burglar alarm activating. The offender was located hiding under a bookcase in the school library. The offender was not bitten.

18th May 1981
A Division

S/V stopped and driver arrested in Bond Street, Bristol. This was a very nasty individual who did not play up too much due to the presence of Major.

13th June 1981
Dragonara Hotel, Redcliffe Way
A Division

A burglary occurred at the Dragonara Hotel in Redcliffe. The offender made off but was stopped and arrested on description in Prewett Street, Redcliffe.

15th June 1981
Dukes of Hazzard
A Division

This job originated in City Road, St Pauls, Bristol. At about 1.30am on this morning I was driving my dog van along City Road, from Ashley Road in the direction of Stokes Croft. As I went across the junction on Brigstocke Road a large motorcycle (two up) passed me at the traffic lights. The motorcycle was heading in the opposite direction to me. As we passed I instinctively looked in my wing mirror and saw the pillion passenger turn around to see if I was going to follow them. My gut reaction was that something was not right, and I decided to turn around and pursue the motorcycle with the intention of stopping it and confirming that everything was in order.

I turned around quite quickly and caught up with the motorcycle in Ashley Road. Both riders were wearing full-face crash helmets.

I turned on my van's blue light to indicate that I wanted the rider to pull in and stop. As soon as the rider realised that he had been compromised he accelerated off at high speed. A chase then ensued all over the division. What I did not know at this time was that this was a £1,000 stolen motorcycle from the Yate area of North Avon. What I also did not know was that both offenders were only fifteen years old, and consequently were quite inexperienced riders. These two youths were wearing denim jeans and jackets, and with their full-face helmets it was impossible to realise that they were only juveniles. It later transpired that they had committed around twenty-five burglaries during a mini crime spree.

However, the chase continued around the division. At the time I was pursuing the villains at about fifty yards distant. Gradually other A Division units joined in the pursuit and other units positioned themselves at the M32 and M4 junctions, just in case the villains should try and escape up the motorway.

As I said, the chase was taking us all over the division, and as we approached the Bear Pit Roundabout near to Debenhams, PC Dave Hitchins, in a marked Panda car, joined in the pursuit. Dave managed to get in front of me, so then we had the stolen motorcycle, followed by Dave Hitchins in his Panda car and me and Major in our dog van. The chase continued along Bond Street and up and across the *Evening Post* roundabout at Temple Way. The stolen motorcycle then roared off down Temple Way towards Avon Street and the bridge that travels across the Floating Harbour.

Suddenly when the bike was going past the IBM Building on Temple Way, it veered off to the right and drove at speed over the central reservation kerb and made towards the Clerical & Medical office building, which was on the opposite side of the road. Dave Hitchins followed suit, and so did I in my dog van. We must have hit that kerb at about thirty-five miles per hour. Firstly, I saw Dave's Panda bounce up in the air over the kerb. Then it was my turn – *wallop! Crash! Bang!* We took off. Major, who was loose, hit the roof of the van and then lurched forward, nearly onto the front passenger seat. How I did not take the steering out I don't know, but worse was to follow.

To be honest, I was really now following Dave Hitchins because he was obscuring my view of the lads on the bike. As we approached the kerb and grass area at the front of Clerical & Medical, little was I to know that Dave and I would soon be airborne. What you have to understand is that the Clerical & Medical building was set back about twenty feet from the grass verge, and that street level was grass kerb level. This grass verge sloped off very steeply and I imagine there was a good ten to twelve-foot drop down this embankment to the underground parking facility below. Before I knew it, Dave had hit the kerb and disappeared down the slope.

Suddenly, with a hell of a bang, I hit the kerb and then – nothing. Time seemed to stand still as my momentum had taken me off the grass, and for a split second Victor Alpha (my call sign) was flying. The split second was enough time for me to think, Oh shit! We are going to come to a sudden halt in a minute! And we did. With a thud we landed sump first and my head hit the rear-view mirror, cutting my forehead.

My dog van windows were open and Major was out looking for blood. He took off on his own accord. As I got out I could see Dave Hitchins running in front of me, and Major closing in on him. I screamed at Dave to stand still. He turned, saw Major closing in and froze. All I can think is that Major must have seen at least one of the villains still running ahead of Dave. The reason I say that is because Major only had a cursory snap at Dave as he charged past him. If Major had had Dave only in his sights he would have nailed him big time.

But Major had vanished. I joined Dave and told him to stay very close to me, but not in front of me. Major had disappeared into the underground car park below the Clerical & Medical and was lost to sight.

From previous experience I had learned not to get too concerned about Major becoming lost because I was confident that as soon as my dog had located the offender, a confirmatory distress call from the said offender would soon be forthcoming.

This in fact was exactly the case, for as we ran out of the basement car park into Cheese Lane we were confronted by a large tanker-type lorry which was parked unattended against the Shot Tower Wall. Suddenly a dreadful, nerve-tingling cry came from the far side of the lorry. Yep – we can confirm, 'one in custody'.

As we went to the side of the lorry I saw that Major had one of the motorcyclists held by the leg. I got Major off this offender and Dave Hitchins took him into custody. My intention now was to carry on with Major and search for the second offender. I shouted out a challenge, basically saying, "This is the police – if you do not show yourself I will release my dog." Suddenly from nowhere a whimpering, pathetic, totally submissive second offender appeared. Apparently, the cries from his accomplice were enough to convince him that a meeting with Major was not the outcome he sought. Both offenders were taken into custody and conveyed to Central.

The first offender had sustained quite serious dog bite wounds and was detained in the Bristol Royal Infirmary for a few days.

There is a little more to this story, as I will explain. During the pursuit, flights and crashes of the Trinity Road spare car and my dog van, quite serious, expensive damage had been caused to both vehicles (not to mention both Dave's and my superficial head injuries).

When a police vehicle is involved in an accident it is termed a POLAC (police accident). This POLAC has to be initially investigated by a supervisory officer (at least a sergeant). On this occasion, due to the complex, extensive nature of the POLAC, the night tour Central Inspector John Clapp was the officer dealing with it.

Now bear in mind both Dave's and my vehicles were down a ten-foot drop into the basement car park of the Clerical & Medical office building. Just prior to Inspector Clapp attending the scene, my dog supervisory (Sgt Ron Pell) attended in Temple Way, parking his marked dog van outside of the Clerical & Medical, more or less level with our two vehicles that were down over the drop into the car park.

Ron had been down with me in the car park, finding out all the facts, checking on my injuries and examining the van. I believe he was then heading to Central and then the BRI to check on the injured offender.

As we made our way around to the front of Clerical & Medical we saw Inspector Clapp pull up with one of his sergeants. Inspector Clapp got out of his car and proceeded to walk around Ron's dog van with his torch, examining the front, back, sides, roof and doors. He was accompanied by his sergeant, who was also studiously examining the van.

Upon seeing us approach, Inspector Clapp said to Ron something like, "I don't know what all the fuss is about, there doesn't seem to be much damage to this one." Ron explained that the van he was inspecting was actually his van, and not the one involved in the POLAC!

Inspector Clapp said, "I thought the POLAC was at the Clerical & Medical in Temple Way – where is the damaged dog van?" Ron then ushered Mr Clapp across the grass verge and pointed over the drop into the void. Below us, you could see the mangled remains of my dog van, Dave's Panda car and the stolen motorcycle.

The look on Inspector Clapp's face was one of utter disbelief and amazement. I am reliably informed that this was possibly the only occasion when anyone ever heard Inspector Clapp swear. He said something like, "How the f*****g hell did that get down there?" The rest is history.

Months later when the youths went to Juvenile Court the Magistrate deemed that the injuries sustained by Offender 1 were sufficient punishment and gave both offenders a conditional discharge or similar minor punishment.

At the commencement of the story I related how their clothing and full-face crash helmets had made it impossible to recognise that these offenders were in fact fifteen-year-old boys. Hindsight is a great thing, and if I had known that these persons were so young, would I have deployed Major? The answer is no.

Diary comment: *Great job – good pick-up.*

Dave Hitchins' Version of this Story

I have been retired seventeen years and probably have not seen Dave Hitchins for twenty-five years. When I decided to write this book I asked NARPO (Bristol & Avon and Somerset branches) to put a message on their respective websites requesting that any former officers with Major anecdotes please contact me. After thirty-four years this is what Dave sent me.

Hi Pete, prompted by a post on Facebook (NARPO) by Keith Jones I'm just emailing a few memories that leap to the front of my mind.

As you will remember your shifts were just about the same pattern as A Division Group 1 (or at least we used to see a lot of you, especially on nights) and Major was the 'kiddie'. A frightening, gorgeous animal he was.

One night shift, I believe it was in the early 80s, during the wee hours you put up a shout that you had chase with an off-road-type motorbike, two up. I was single-crewed in the little Talbot Sunbeam (the 'rabbit hutch'), which was a nippy little car and was the spare incident car (Alpha-Tango Five-Zero) at Trinity.

Listening to the chase, I picked the bike up ahead and waited just off the top roundabout near Debenhams and took the lead from you. I was going at a fair lick but the chase didn't last long because we all ended up going through Old Market underpass towards Temple Meads, and then the bike suddenly jumped the central kerb and veered off across the opposite lane, over the pavement onto the grassed area outside the Clerical & Medical building, and then over a very steep slope where it crashed at the bottom. I wasn't going to let them get away so I followed suit, crossing the central kerb with a huge 'crunch' (I dread to think what damage it caused to the underside of the car!), then across the grass and realised – oh shit! – that with the slope and the speed I was doing, I was going to be airborne.

I lost as much speed as I could but there was a brief moment when time stood still. I had four wheels off the ground and I was flying. There was a sinking feeling in my gut, then… bang! I landed, my head lurched forward and I banged my forehead on the rear-view mirror. All my kit and bits and pieces flew all around inside the car. I knew the car must have had a bit of damage, as I remember in slow motion the illuminated police sign and the blue light, with its last dying flicker, flying off the roof down the windscreen, bouncing on the bonnet and then on to oblivion, trailing wires behind it.

The two lads on the motorcycle were still down on the ground as I landed and I must have missed them by inches.

I think they were mortified/electrified by what they had seen and had not expected the police to follow, but in a split second they were galvanised and were up and running through an underground car park beneath the Clerical & Medical towards Cheese Lane (near the Bush lead-shot tower). I had to literally kick open my car door to get out (the chassis had obviously bent/buckled and the door was jammed); then I was out running after the fugitives. As I got out I heard what I thought was a kamikaze aircraft above me, about to crash. Looking around I saw your white dog van fully airborne, headlamps and blue lights blazing, but coming in at a very steep landing angle, i.e. nose first…then, crash! You had arrived!

All this happened within just a few seconds, and I continued running through the dark underground car park chasing after the two lads, who were about twenty yards ahead. Suddenly, I heard your shout: "Stop, stand still for f**** sake, Dave! Stand still… Major is out… Stop!"

I then remember a cold shiver ran through me. I instantly froze to the spot in the dark and put my hands on my head (I learned later from you that Major had jumped out of the van window and set off on his own in a very bad mood after the crash landing). I stood there in abject terror, fearing the legendary 'werewolf'. I thought Major was about to disembowel me or worse; I could hear him running from behind me and letting out the most terrifying barks, which were amplified and echoed in the underground car park (I don't know what was loudest: the sound of my heartbeat or Major's bark.) I glanced backwards, afraid to move, and saw him closing in and thought, Oh God, I'm dead!

It was like some horror movie, like The Werewolf of London – all I could make out were glowing eyes and massive glinting teeth wrapped in a mass of black and tan fuzz, closing in at an incredible rate. I closed my eyes and waited for Armageddon. Then there were more shouted commands from you to leave, or whatever you said. He passed by me, but at the same time snapped at me. I remember the sound of his teeth clashing to my right as he aimed his gnashers at my leg. I could feel the snap of his teeth, which were millimetres from connecting. I was a lucky boy!

I was frozen to the spot for a few seconds; then you ran past me and I followed. The lads had exited into Cheese Lane and were lost to sight, as was Major. Then I heard the most blood-curdling screams I've ever heard from someone up ahead in the dark, and a deep, snarling growl which accompanied them.

The screaming and snarling was up ahead, but following the sound (you in the lead of course) it led up to an HGV parked on the left, close to a wall (I think it was some sort of tanker vehicle), and you shone a torch into the gap between the lorry and the wall…OMG! Major had got his man alright.

You managed to get Major off and out and into his lead, then we extracted the youth who had a bit of a bite (a slight understatement) to his leg. I was expanding but you know the details, and whilst I looked after the detained lad you set off after lad number two, calling out something like, "Come out or I'll release the dog", whilst at the same time Major was barking his head off.

Needless to say, following the ungodly screams given out by lad number one the second lad saw sense and came out from hiding in the grounds of the 'Pip 'n' Jay' churchyard, crying out for mercy.

Two in custody and a double POLAC. The arrival of Inspector John Clapp at the scene was the decider that made us both too unwell to be spoken to until after we had been treated for our 'crash injuries'. The hospital story and thereafter…well, that's the next chapter.

8th July 1981

This incident centred around a boy and girl having an argument at Gilda Parade up on the Wells Road at Whitchurch, South Bristol. What was originally thought to have been an attempted burglary, in truth turned out to be the plate glass window of a chemist smashed by an irate boyfriend after a row.

Criminal damage of about £500 had been caused and the offender had been chased by officers, but lost in an area of dense undergrowth. The area had been sealed off and the bobbies sensibly awaited my arrival.

Normally upon my arrival I would have challenged the area by shouting something like, "This is the police, come out now before I release the dog." I would then after a short wait release Major, and he would locate anyone hiding in the area (if they were still there). Normally, indications would usually be the sound of the police dog barking loudly.

Major's indications were somewhat different. It's a fact that a dog cannot bark when it has an arm or leg grasped tightly between its jaws; therefore, I waited for offenders to scream. There was quite a high chance that Major would probably attack whoever he found hiding in the bushes. The incident at the Clerical & Medical building was still fresh in my mind, and I truthfully did not want anyone injured unnecessarily. Therefore, when I turned up, my challenge was somewhat prolonged and sincere. I had Major out of the van, at my side and on his lead, and as normal he was barking loudly and aggressively. Even though B Division was not my normal area of patrol, Major's reputation was city-wide and no officer in his right mind stood within ten yards of us.

This email anecdote from ex-Inspector Paul Stephens confirms what I said: Major truly was a legend!

Hello Pete, just seen the item on the NARPO website regarding your book. Major was a legend in his time and I will certainly be able to send you some background on a couple of his exploits on B Division (including *that* detective nibble).

So on this occasion, my challenge went something like this: "This is the police here. I have a police dog here that I will release to find you if you do not give yourself up. There is the distinct possibility you could be injured. For a broken window it's just not worth it."

Initially, there was no response, so I waited. During this time Major was yelping and barking; however, to increase his 'bad attitude', I gave him the left knee shoulder nudge. This was his trigger to unleash hell. He went ballistic, barking, growling and snorting, mainly at the B Division officers, who were gradually easing further back. Major was up on his hind legs with his lips curled so far back you could almost see the directions to A&E tattooed on his gums.

Believe it or not, this had the desired effect. Suddenly, a voice was heard coming from the middle of the bushes. Someone was yelling, "Keep the dog there, I'm coming out. Is the dog safe? I don't want any trouble." With that, I put Major back in the van and once assured that he was put away, the offender emerged from the bushes and was taken into custody. Nice arrest with no one injured.

Diary comment: *Wish they were all like this.*

9th July 1981
Haymarket, Broadmead
A Division

This was a shop burglary. The offender ran off and was detained.

12th July 1981
Christmas Steps, Bristol Central

A man wearing a top with green arrows smashed a window of the Post Office and ran off. He was arrested on description outside of the Colston Hall.

15th July 1981
A Division
Road Traffic Accident

Failed to stop RTA in the city centre, right in front of me. I had no option but a quick pursuit and then positive breath test (I only ever gave six in my entire police career). The driver was drunk and a danger to everyone.

8th August 1981
B Division
A group of punks assaulted a man in Totterdown. The villain was found hiding in the Central Trading Estate. A nasty little punk was nicked.

15th October 1981
A Division
A motorcar had been broken into by two youths in High Kingsdown. Two were arrested and stolen property was recovered from where they were nicked (house doorway).

30th October 1981
Western Services Garage, Pennywell Road, Easton, Bristol
Note: this was the only offender Major ever bit on the forearm (i.e. as in training). This was a professional criminal doing a not-so-professional safe-breaking job.

Although I was on nights and attended the job at about 2am, the entire process began a lot earlier, at around 4pm.

The attacked premises was quite a large garage and office complex in Pennywell Road, Bristol, and it had a large car park which contained lots of vehicles of all sorts. On a Saturday afternoon around 4pm the police received the first reports of banging coming from within the premises. I was told that the original unit attending heard no noises and that the premises were locked and secure. Why they never followed up with keyholders I don't know. During the evening there were apparently further calls about banging and hammering coming from the garage, and I am told this was explained as, "It's a garage, that's what they do, they bang and hammer. Yes, they make a noise."

When the banging continued well past midnight a sergeant at Trinity Road decided to investigate a little more thoroughly. I was called in at about 2am and what we discovered was amazing.

A well-known South Bristol safe-breaker had actually been in the main office of the premises, trying his hardest to literally break into the company safe. He must have been smashing away at this huge safe for hours with sledgehammers and a lump hammer.

He had managed to get the back steel plate off the safe; however, then he encountered a mass of reinforced concrete. The mess in the office was unbelievable: tiny chunks of cement and concrete were everywhere.

I had seen safes in the past that had been breached with thermic lances, and that really was effective and professional. This was just one huge pile of mess.

I had made a search of the offices when we first arrived, which was negative. We all assumed that our safe-breaker had literally worn himself out and had left without ever cracking the safe. In earlier recollections, I emphasised the point of persevering and not giving up to soon and how patience really can be a virtue.

Well, I decided to have a scout around the rather large perimeter fence of this complex. You never know what might turn up. It was whilst I was out on the far side of the compound that an urgent shout came over the radio. The gist of the message was that an officer thought he had seen a figure thirty feet up on the roof of the office block that had been burgled. By the time I ran around to the correct side I caught sight of two figures on the roof. There was a police officer gingerly making his way along the side of the roof and another figure (I presume our Mr Safe-Breaker) was moving a little faster away from the officer, but the safe-breaker was heading to the far edge of the roof, and there was nowhere to go, or so we all thought.

Suddenly Mr Safe-Breaker was gone. I am told that he leapt from about thirty feet into the large car park below that was packed full of vehicles. Mr Safe-Breaker had disappeared in amongst all of the vehicles. Now this is where Major and I came into our own. This was a large car park with dozens of vans, cars and small lorries crammed into it. The place was surrounded by a chain-link fence and we had it secure.

I stood at the gate to the compound and said to Major, whilst he was still on his lead, "Where is he?" Plus, I gave him the knee-in-the-shoulder trigger to let him know it was time to go to work. I released him and off he charged, growling as he went. He disappeared in amongst the cars and vans, reappearing for a second, his tail up like a scorpion's, ready to strike, up and down the rows of cars again, darting in and out, whining as he went, then away again out of sight in amongst the lorries.

Then away in front of me about seven or eight vehicles up I heard a cry; someone, no doubt Mr Safe-Breaker, was screaming, "Get him off!"

I ran between the cars just in time to see Major dragging out a well-known South Bristol villain by his forearm from under a transit-type van. Major was really giving the guy's arm some serious attention. Luckily for him he had a thickish jacket on, and quite a lot of Major's venom was being absorbed by the jacket.

Eventually, Major succeeded in dragging Mr Safe-Breaker out from under the van. I managed to get the dog off him and he was taken into custody via the BRI.

His hospital visit on this occasion was not merely down to Major; bearing in mind this guy jumped from a standing position of about thirty feet onto tarmac. The rumours were that he had broken both his ankles in the jump from the roof. I don't know if this was correct but he certainly seemed in more pain from his ankles than from his arm.

This was the first and only ever time Major bit anyone on the forearm. Mr Safe-Breaker –professional that he was – made no complaint whatsoever about his dog bites.

Diary comment: *Excellent nick.*

2nd November 1981
Rear of Gateway Supermarket, North Road, St Andrews, Bristol C Division

Three men were arrested on the roof of Gateway. One offender had a crowbar, and was nicked for going equipped for theft.

3rd November 1981
Armed robbery at KFC in Bedminster, Bristol
B Division

The offender had been stopped by the police about three hundred yards from KFC. I tracked from KFC to the offender. There was a £5 note found on the track. The offender was armed with a knife.

A guilty plea and four-year sentence were issued at Newport Crown Court. I believe he had further offences outstanding from Gwent Police.

Diary comment: *Nice confirmatory track and cash found.*

27th November 1981
Pennywell Road, Easton, Bristol

A smash-and-grab at an electrical shop in Pennywell Road. Two offenders were found hiding in the shop doorway.

30th November 1981
Temple Meads Railway Club, Bristol
A Division

The railway club was burgled and Major chased and pursued the two offenders into the arms of waiting BTP officers. They never knew how lucky they were to have kept ahead of Major. He flushed them out and there were no bites.

1st December 1981
Arley Hill, Cotham, Bristol

S/V, a motorcycle crashed and offender ran off from the police. PD Major tracked a very short distance and found the offender hiding in bushes.

A nice little easy-track villain, not bitten.

24th January 1982
Celestian Textiles, Victoria Parade, St George, Bristol

There was a burglary at a commercial premises. Three offenders were in the building. PD Major located two criminals in an office.

The third offender was arrested by PS Essex (dog sergeant).

Diary comment: *Good job – I nicked two, Vernon got number three who tried to run away.*

24th January 1982
City Road, St Pauls, Bristol
A Division

What was quite unusual about this particular job was that it was only about an hour after we had arrested two burglars in St George.

This job concerned a guy who was holding his girlfriend and their very young baby hostage in a barricaded flat. Remembering all the facts is difficult; however, I do recall that at some point we knew the girl and baby were definitely in another room, and at a given signal the door was smashed in and Major and I entered and took the offender down.

Diary comment: *Good solid dog job.*

7th February 1982
Philadelphia Court, Broadmead, Bristol

Three persons were seen acting suspiciously at night around the rear of the shops. All three located were in possession of tools and were nicked on suspicion of going equipped for theft.

21st February 1982
South Liberty Lane, Ashton, Bristol
B Division

Five youths had been disturbed while causing criminal damage at the far end of South Liberty Lane in Ashton, Bristol. I cannot recall what they had damaged but I do remember that Major tracked two up onto Bedminster Down, where he located them near to the Bristol Water Company, hiding in undergrowth. The track was up and over the railway lines and must have been nearly a mile in length. I recall one offender getting a nip off Major. It was a very good track, but unfortunately three villains got away.

22nd February 1982
An Address in Whitchurch, South Bristol
B Division

A suspect's stolen car was abandoned in the middle of the night in Whitchurch, South Bristol.

One youth had run off and was lost to sight. I arrived with Major and he quickly led me a short distance into the garden of a house some two hundred yards away – he had tracked the villain. This house transpired to be the home of a well-known criminal family. They had quite a fearsome reputation and were not averse to fighting with the police.

As I went into the rear garden of this address Major immediately went to the locked door of an outside shed and started barking loudly and aggressively.

Almost immediately three men came out of the house and became very abusive and aggressive. Two were men in their twenties and one was presumably the father in his fifties.

I was joined by other officers and a sort of Mexican standoff ensued. To me it was obvious that the person who had run away from the stolen car was most definitely in the shed. It was also obvious that these two men did not want the police entering the shed.

I can recall that it was a cold winter's night but I'm sure the two younger men had just jeans on and no tops. I remember thinking a few things: 1) they must be bloody cold and 2) someone's going to get bitten in a minute. I was correct.

From what I can recall the Broadbury Road supervisory said, "Put the shed door in." This was duly kicked open and Major went into say hello to Mr Car Thief. You know very well what happened: silly Mr Car Thief kicked Major (honestly not a good idea) and Major duly attacked him and decided not to let go.

A big fight then began with the brothers and father of the car thief attacking the police. All hell was let loose for a few minutes and once my prisoner had been detached from Major and placed in custody in a police car, Major bit a few other bad guys until all four were nicked.

That was not the end of the story. Quite a few months later all the family appeared in Crown Court, and a fair bit of unpleasantness was experienced in the public areas. The family's friends and supporters played up no end.

Quite a number of complaints were made against the police, in particular Major and me. I have no idea how the trial ended because after giving evidence I left.

Diary comment: *Very nasty people.*

23rd February 1982
Church Road, Redfield, Bristol
A Division

The thief was caught stealing a letter from under the shop door. He ran off from the police. Major located him in a local car sales plot.

14th April 1982
College Green, Bristol
A Division

Two persons acting suspiciously turned out to be absconders from a care home in Bristol.

16th April 1982
Prince Street, City Docks
A Division

This was a silly little job. I nicked two yobs who had decided to throw traffic signs and road repair lamps into the docks.

16th April (the Same Night)
Princess Victoria Street
C Division

Two yobs broke into washing machines to nick the coins. They were caught in the act.

17th April 1982
Sevier Street, St Pauls, Bristol
A Division

Two women were nicked for damaging police cars.

20th April 1982
St Mary on the Quay, City Centre
A Division

An absconder from a borstal in Wiltshire.

29th April 1982
Baptist Mills School
A Division

A missing female was located.

30th April 1982
Wheatsheaf Pub, Nelson Street, Bristol
A Division

A nasty wounding; one male arrested.

2nd June 1982
Chipping Sodbury
D Division

The reason I recall this job so vividly is because we were on a day's training on the Portbury 100s (the road that runs parallel to the M5 northbound), just down from the Gordano motorway services. There had been a theft of jewellery from premises in Chipping Sodbury out in South Gloucestershire, and the local unit believed that the offender who had been chased had gone to ground in the vicinity of a court-yard just off the High Street. The duty day dog was already tied up on a job over in Knowle West and Force Control were asking for any dog unit to attend. I duly responded, and with my twos and blues full-on I zoomed the seventeen miles to the job. Upon my arrival, true to their word, the local units had secured a large area of land at the rear of the High Street. It didn't take Major too long to locate the offender, who was concealed right in the middle of a huge, dense bramble bush, together with the stolen watches in his pockets. This guy was in his fifties and a professional criminal. He was scratched to hell but would have been prepared to hide there until dark if necessary.

Diary comment: *D Div. good setup and nice little find.*

10th June 1982
Little Bishop Street, Easton, Bristol

The reason I can recall this job so well is because of the two extremely nasty villains that were involved. At the risk of repeating this fact, do you recall how I said that I like to search premises alone if possible? There may be an odd occasion where you need the keyholder with you, but I personally did not want any other copper in with me either cocking up the search or, to be honest, finding Mr Burglar.

Well, on this occasion I believe that a bleeper alarm had been installed in an office block that we had reason to suspect was going to be broken into. A bleeper can be a thin pressure mat concealed under another mat or carpet, and is only activated when pressure (body weight) is applied to it.

There had been a silent approach by all units to the offices in question, which were surrounded and a forced door was located at the rear. No audible alarm was sounding, so the villains most likely did not know that the old bill were in attendance.

I cannot recall how I kept Major quiet, but I did, and we duly entered the building and again for some reason that I can't recall, I kept him on his lead.

As I searched the dark corridors I heard voices coming from a distant office. The time for silence was over and I burst into this room with a very bright Dragon Light (a powerful torch).

Major's knee switch was activated and he went into overdrive. I was shouting and screaming, "Police, police, do not move or he will do you." Major was doing the business big time and was snarling and growling with 100% venom and intent; he really did look and sound like he could inflict some serious injury if you called his bluff.

In front of us were two well-known, very tasty villains; they were both in their mid-thirties, and had convictions for violence plus assault on police. I think that they were so surprised and overwhelmed by Major's actions that they offered no resistance at all. I was quickly joined by other officers, who took them both into custody.

One of them could not resist the sneer and comment as he

passed me in cuffs: "Just as well you had the dog", and yes, it was just as well that I had a dog like Major, because I think if I had had poor little Dena with me then I may have been on a loser!

Diary comment: *Good job.*

11th July 1982
Bristol City Centre

This was a nothing little job where we had a large fight in the city centre adjacent to the taxi rank. Whilst trying to separate the two warring factions, one silly individual who was playing to the ladies in the taxi queue refused to move on and was duly arrested for obstruction. No bites and no injuries.

23rd July 1982
Entertainment Centre, Frogmore Street, Bristol
A Division

Three yobs assaulted a youth and made off. Two were detained and charged. They were found hiding in Culver Street.

8th August 1982
Christmas Steps, City Centre, Bristol
A Division

A youth was arrested for assaulting a club doorman.

3rd October 1982
B Division

A stolen car was chased and abandoned in the Whitchurch area of city. The offender was located hiding in gardens.

4th October 1982
Fishponds Road, Bristol
B Division

A burglar was disturbed and ran off. He was located in the water treatment works at Eastville, Bristol.

21st October 1982
Temple Way
A Division
A road traffic accident involving a stolen vehicle; three ran off. They
were three very nasty crooks from B Division who were located
hiding nearby and arrested.

29th October 1982
"Walked Straight Into My Arms"
Belmont Street, Easton, Bristol
A Division – Nights
The following case involved patience, perseverance and a huge slice
of luck, or in the case of the burglar that I arrested, bad luck.

The time was about 3am; however, the job that I was on, in the
Belmont Road/St Mark's Road area, occurred a good hour earlier
and in all honesty had absolutely nothing to do with the prisoner
that I was about to arrest.

At around 2am a youth had been disturbed while breaking
into a car in St Mark's Road, Easton, Bristol. He had run off prior
to police attending and was lost to sight in the vicinity of the
Stapleton Road Railway Station. I had no joy with the track or
search, and because it was a quiet night I decided to turn my radio
down and just mooch around on foot with Major on his lead in
the general area.

Sometimes it pays to just sit quiet and watch for a reaction. Dogs
can hear frequencies of 40Hz to 60KHz; the human hearing range
is only 12Hz to 20KHz. Dogs use up to eighteen muscles to move
their ears, which enables them to locate and pinpoint sounds far
more precisely than we humans can. It is believed that dogs can hear
sounds up to four times further away than humans, so by sitting
quiet and letting your dog do the work you can benefit. (This sitting
still, listening and waiting was once described by my old sergeant
John Broadbelt as masterful inactivity.)

A textbook on dogs I once read said that if a dog suddenly turns
his head upon hearing a sound, if you were to take a line from the

centre of its ear you would pinpoint the location of the sound.

Also, a dog's sense of smell is amazing. The olfactory membrane (the part of the brain that deals with smells) is about forty times larger in a dog than in a human. A dog's sense of smell is anywhere between one thousand and ten million times more sensitive than a human's (depending upon the breed). Apparently a human has around five million scent glands, whereas a dog has anywhere between 125 million and 300 million. (At this point I did wonder how they actually counted these glands.) These amazing statistics explain why a dog can follow a scent trail across land, whilst the likes of you and I could sniff the ground all day long and be none the wiser as to where a villain had gone.

I had been sitting around St Mark's Road and Belmont Street for about an hour, and nothing. Then this happened: I was sat on a wall in Belmont Street about seventy yards from the pedestrian exit out from Stapleton Road Railway Station. I had not even seen this guy and he certainly had not seen us; however, Major had. Suddenly a horrible low growl started to grow deep down in his belly. On looking up I saw a young man dressed in a tracksuit and wearing a cap walking out of the station. He was carrying a large flip-top waste bin in both arms. I was about to close in on him when Major started barking aggressively. I was about fifty yards from this guy. Upon seeing us, he turned around and thought about running. Major was by now in full battle cry, and was doing his best to wake up the whole of East Bristol.

I shouted out, "Don't do it!" Thank goodness, this guy immediately saw sense and saved himself a visit to A&E and probably weeks of agony and pain.

I told him to sit down on the pavement and he complied. He was very concerned about the dog, and so was I. I called up a Trinity unit who R/V with us. He took my van keys and his co-driver brought my van around, and Major was safely caged and no one was bitten.

Matey Boy had been caught and the whole story was then conveyed to us. Firstly, he was an absconder from borstal. He had broken into a hardware store near Bell Hill, Stapleton. He had nicked as many high-value goodies as the flip-top bin could carry and then made his way to the railway line at Glenfrome Road. Once upon the railway line, detection was very unlikely. He had walked all along the quiet tracks; I don't think he ever was confronted by a train at all. When he got to Stapleton Road Railway Station he was about three hundred yards from home. He said that as he walked out and saw us, he couldn't believe it. For a split second he said he did think about doing a runner, but then common sense and self-preservation instincts quickly kicked in. He was returned to borstal and had six months added to his sentence.

31st October 1982
Sapphire Theatre Productions, Old Market Street, Bristol
A Division

A smash-and-grab had occurred in a fancy dress hire shop. Two youths had been seen running off carrying items. Upon searching the area, I saw two youths, who upon seeing me dumped what they were carrying. Two were arrested on suspected theft. A number of animal masks were recovered nearby.

3rd November 1982
Old Duke Public House, King Street, Central Bristol
A Division – Nights

This popular pub had a window smashed by a gang of rowdy youths who made off. Five were detained and admitted at Bristol Bridge.

24th November 1983
Burglary – Two Escaped From Fairfax House Department Store in Central Bristol
A Division – Nights

Before I begin this story, I want to quickly tell you about an incident that happened whilst my wife and I were cruising on P&O *Britannia* in June 2015.

It was on about the second day, when we were at sea heading down the coast of Portugal, that a guy about my age (I am now sixty-two, but I look about thirty-seven) approached me and said, "Excuse me, but does the name Major mean anything to you?" I looked at him quizzically and he said, "You obviously don't recognise me," and no, I didn't. The mystery was soon solved when he told me that his name was Joe Murphy, that he was an ex-copper from Bristol, and that in 1982 I had nicked two burglars that had escaped from him at Fairfax House in Bristol. I had not seen him for thirty years – what a coincidence!

The idea of writing my book had been in my mind for years, and when I met Joe and he explained in more detail his version of what happened on that night in Fairfax Street, my resolve to write *A Job With Bite* was more fixed than ever.

The events that night went something like this: at around 2.30am on that winter's night on 24th November 1982, an A1 (burglar alarm) had been received from Fairfax House in Fairfax Street, Bristol.

Now Fairfax House, I believe, was part of the Co-op group. It was a large, long, narrow store about six floors in height. It was a department store that sold almost everything. Its position was on the edge of the Broadmead shopping centre. Opposite Fairfax House on the non-Broadmead side were Castle Park and the old St Peter's Church. Castle Park is quite a large open space. Beyond the far side of the Castle Park was a twenty-foot drop into a portion of the Bristol Floating Harbour. A wall and railings were adequate to prevent anyone accidentally falling into the harbour.

On the night in question, the bobbies turned up and surrounded Fairfax House as best they could and awaited the keyholder. As stated, it was a long building with a number of entrances, fire exits and a goods entrance in Fairfax Street.

I do not know from where in the building they exited, but I suspect it was a ground-floor fire exit on the Castle Park side. The villains would have run across Newgate and been lost to sight on entering Castle Park.

I know that Joe had seen them break out of the store, but I believe that he was too far away to apprehend them. What happened next was that the shout was up: "Two out and running." Adrenaline kicked in and no doubt cops would have been swarming over Castle Park in minutes.

With the best of intentions, they probably sent mobile units to the extremities of Castle Park to hopefully contain the situation and ensure that the villains remained in the vicinity of Castle Park. Foot bobbies had no doubt flooded Castle Park and begun searching St Peter's Church, the bandstand and all the other nooks and crannies that occur in and around that area of parkland.

I attended from quite some distance away; I believe that I had been on a shout to Avonmouth, so it took me a good fifteen minutes to get to the scene. Upon my arrival I had a brief chat with local officers (presumably Joe Murphy). I got the gist of the job and learned that two offenders had made off into Castle Park.

I could see torch lights flashing and glimmering all over Castle Park as bobbies scoured every bush. The possibility of a track was out of the question due to the presence of so many coppers. However, what I did suggest was that with the exception of the officers positioned around the perimeter, I wanted to withdraw all officers from Castle Park, wait a while for things to quieten down and for all of that police scent to dissipate, and then Major and I alone would search the park. Consultations were had with the divisional supervisory officer and this action plan was duly agreed.

It was now well gone 3am; a good thirty minutes had elapsed since the villains had broken out of the store and made good their escape. Now one of two things must have occurred: 1) they had indeed transited across the park and made it out the other side before police sealed it off, or 2) they had gone to ground nearby and had not yet been discovered.

I firstly made sure that all of the perimeter bobbies were aware that very shortly Major would be unleashed to commence searching. All of them were either in or very close to a police car should they require urgent refuge.

I began my search at the nearest point to Fairfax House on Castle Park. It's amazing how many fleeing criminals seeking to hide do so almost immediately. This can be a good ploy if PC Plod zooms straight past that first hiding place in his enthusiasm to catch the thief.

With Major it was a simple knee-on-the-shoulder trigger as I let him off the lead, with the FIRM whispered command of, "Where is he, then?" Off he dashed. He was keen, he was excited, he was on the hunt and he knew it. Excitedly sniffing bushes, shrubs, in fact everywhere. I was doing my best to keep him in sight, but it wasn't easy. As we progressed into Castle Park, I decided to concentrate in and around St Peter's Church. There were lots of hidey-holes in and around the church and we searched them all, with a negative result.

I was constantly keeping the A Division radio control informed of how and where we were progressing. This was for their information and also to hopefully keep the perimeter coppers from straying into my search area and possibly encountering Major.

The church was cleared and we moved on, little by little. The great thing about Major was that he didn't get fed up, tired or complacent. On and on we searched. I imagine it was now approaching thirty minutes since we started, but still we carried on. By now we were up at the top end of the park near to where the bandstand was, up by the Holiday Inn, and still nothing.

It was getting to the point where the majority of open grassy areas had been covered, and it was all negative. I was beginning to wonder if these two scrotes had in fact made it across the park before it was sealed off.

I was now approaching the footpath which leads along the top of the river from what was the ambulance station down towards Bristol Bridge and Baldwin Street. This path is about twenty feet above the river, and I thought, Well, that's it then! I had walked about eighty yards along this path, and to my left was a stone wall about four feet high, with a metal rail on top. The wall was covered with vegetation that had grown up and around it from the river below. There were no signs of anyone anywhere. There was only the wall and the drop down to the river on my left.

As Major and I slowly walked the path, he suddenly stopped. He pushed past me, possibly ten feet or so, and then put his front legs up on the wall and started taking air deeply into his nose. I looked down over the wall, through the bushes and vegetation that festooned the wall, but all I could see was the water about twenty feet below. Because of the angle and all the bushes, I could not see close up against the wall. I could hear nothing. I did think of rats or cats for a second.

I called Major off the wall, walked away about twenty yards and said to him, "Where is he then?" Immediately he returned to the wall, feet up and head swaying as he inhaled deeply. At one point, I was worried that he might try and jump the wall. Major would not leave that patch of wall.

I radioed A Division and was joined in a few minutes by the central supervisory. I explained that I had searched the park with a total negative result, except for this instance of Major's feet up on the wall, indicating the river below. Every time I got him away from the wall and then released him, Major did exactly the same: feet up on the wall, snorting the air.

The Central sergeant then made a quick call and authorised the use of one of the police launches from the River Station at The Grove, about half a mile down the Floating Harbour.

Within around twenty minutes the launch was on the station below us on the water, and we could hear voices. The two burglars from Fairfax House had somehow clambered down the vines and were partly submerged in the water, right up close against the wall. They were suffering from the initial stages of hypothermia.

They were later charged and admitted the job. They were two brothers who really thought that they had got away with it, although they did say they didn't know how much longer they would have survived in that cold November water.

Fantastic job, dog – could not have done it without Major.

Diary comment: *Brilliant work by dog.*

8th January 1983
Fallodon Way, Henleaze, Bristol

This was a stolen car, four up, being chased by C Division officers. It was abandoned in Fallodon Way, Henleaze and the four villains made off through gardens.

Upon my arrival I commenced a search of the gardens in Fallodon Way and Major quickly found one youth hiding behind a shed. The youth was not bitten.

Diary comment: *Nice easy nick.*

22nd February 1983
Burglary, Wholesale Tobacconist, Kellaway Avenue, Horfield, Bristol C Division

It was around 1.30am on 22nd February 1983. A call was received to the effect that an A1 (burglar alarm) had activated at Nash's Wholesale Tobacconists in Kellaway Avenue, Bristol. A local police unit was very close to the shop. The first C Division unit at the scene saw an unidentified person about seventy yards away, running around a corner out of sight. Upon stopping at Nash's he discovered that the entire front window had been smashed in and cartons of various cigarettes were strewn all across the large, wide footway in front of the shop.

Enquiries from the owner later confirmed that approximately seventy thousand cigarettes had been stolen. Upon my arrival at the scene I had a quick chat with the first officer on the scene, and then went to where the unidentified youth had last been seen. I was only about ten minutes behind the initial call, but as I recall it was quite a wet, horrible night. Upon getting to the corner of Cairns Road I put Major on his tracking harness in an effort to locate a track, but to no avail. It was raining quite hard and any trace of a scent on the pavement was literally getting washed away.

I then made the decision to begin searching the back lanes and gardens of houses in the Cairns Road/Russell Road vicinity.

Two things happen when villains run away from a crime scene:

1. If there aren't many cops about, they will keep on running. The greater the distance that they can put between the scene of the crime and themselves, the better. In a city of pavements, it makes hard surface tracking over a long distance very difficult. However, out in the country or over grass in fields, you can successfully track for miles.

2. The other option the villain has is to hide. To go to ground ASAP, to hide up, wait for the law to leave and then blend in with the early morning workers/dog walkers, etc.

I have known some villains wait up for hours, sometimes falling asleep in the process. The one good thing about the ploy from a dog handler's point of view is that whilst they are holed up, they are continually giving off scent and creating a larger, more intense scent profile for the dog to locate and home in on.

It was now about 1.45, and I was with Major, going in and out of the rear gardens, up and down the back lanes in an attempt to locate one or more of the burglars from a wholesale tobacconist. It was still raining but this had no detrimental effect on Major as he was in hunting mode. He was in and out of gardens, jumping over walls, sniffing and snorting at every door, shed or outside toilet that he came across. His tail was in the upright scorpion position. It was wet but he did not care a jot. This was work; this was what he loved to do.

We had been searching dozens of gardens when suddenly his demeanour changed slightly. It seemed to go up a gear as we entered this particular garden: his ears pricked up, his tail stiffened even more, and I instinctively whispered to him, "Go on, where is he then?" With that, he was at the door of what was either an outside toilet or a shed belonging to one of the terraced houses in Russell Road. Major was snorting and sniffing at the doorjamb and the gap at the bottom of the door. Suddenly he got very excited and aggressive and started barking and growling, pawing at the door. I tried the door – it wasn't locked, but bodily pressure was stopping me from opening it. I thought we had one of our burglars hiding inside.

I tried again a little more forcefully as I shouted, "Police! Come out now or else the door is going in."

A voice from behind the door then shouted out, "OK, OK, but I'm not coming out until that dog is safe." I then radioed in my location and situation and within minutes I was joined in the garden by C Division officers.

I had Major safely on his lead and well back when a very well-known young criminal emerged from the outhouse. He was cuffed and immediately taken into custody, denying any involvement in the cigarette burglary. This was in the age of the skinhead and our suspect was dressed in cropped denim jeans, high, twelve-hole red Dr Marten bovver boots and a T-shirt and denim jacket. His hair was a very short skinhead style.

I believe that others were involved in the burglary (after all, seventy thousand cigarettes had been nicked), but they had made good their escape.

Now we needed to find the stolen cigarettes. I returned to Redland nick for a chat with night CID who confirmed that around seventy thousand cigarettes had in fact been stolen from Nash's. In 1983 twenty cigarettes were about £1.05. The value of the alleged stolen property was about £3,500. In today's market with a packet of twenty costing £8, the value would probably be over £25,000.

The night D/C said, "We've got to look about to see if we can find these cigarettes."

I've got to be honest, I was thinking these guys obviously had a van. It was a dreadful night; they wouldn't have walked there. The nicked fags were probably in a van and gone long before the law arrived upon the scene.

Nevertheless, I returned to the Kellaway Avenue/Cairns Road vicinity and started mooching around with Major off his lead. It was now gone 4am and the roads were still deserted. I could let Major have a free rein without the worry of him bumping into anyone.

To say I was searching was not a lie because I had my eye out looking for the cartons of stolen cigarettes (10 x packs of 20, making a carton = 200 ciggies). However, if I'm honest we were both mooching about. I kept telling myself that to persevere and not give up easily was the hallmark of a good dog handler. At least it had stopped raining.

It was most probably a good half-hour that we had been swanning around when we came upon a triangular area of single-storey lock-up garages off Halsbury Road, which is off Cairns Road in Bishopston, Bristol.

As I stood at the open entrance to this triangle of garages, I honestly thought there was nothing or no one here and I could see every garage. There was nowhere to hide. I couldn't be bothered to walk up around every garage, so I sent Major with a quick whisper of, "Where is he then?" Off he charged, still full of enthusiasm.

He charged up one side, sniffing as he went. He carried on down the second side of the triangle, but then slowed and in fact turned around and went back to a locked and secure garage right up the end of the row on the right-hand side. I didn't know what to think. He didn't bark or show aggression, but he just wouldn't leave this particular garage door. Sod it! I thought. I would have to go up and investigate myself. If this is a bloody cat, Major, you will swing for it.

As I approached the garage I could see that it had two wooden doors and a hasp and padlock securing it. Major was prancing up and down, looking at the garage then looking at me, back and forth. As I got up to the garage I could see that there was a good two-inch gap between the doors. Yes, there was a metal hasp and padlock securing the door.

When I shone my Maglite torch through the gap I was absolutely astounded at what I saw. There was a large, old Jaguar car inside, with no engine and no bonnet. In the void where the engine compartment was were lots and lots and lots of cartons of cigarettes. I could not believe it!

I have said before in these pages that Major was good, but on my life, this dog was magnificent.

Night CID turned up, we forced the door and the whole garage was full of the nicked fags from Nash's.

The next bit really pissed me off, though: I did not get off duty until nearly 8am. The following night I had a message at Bower to call in at Redland CID office to see the night D/C. I presumed that he just wanted to clarify a few points about the cigarette job. When I got to the CID office at the top of Redland nick I was met by the D/C who handed me a bottle of whisky that was 95% empty. There were the dregs of about half an inch of whisky in the bottom.

He said, "The propriator of the tobacconist brought this for the good work we did."

I said "We?!" The whole job was down to Major. Without him there was no prisoner, no recovered cigarettes; in fact, no job.

The had drunk all of the whisky! Most of them had had nothing to do with the job. I told the DC to stick his whisky "where the sun don't shine" and to tell his detective buddies that they should have bought Major a pound of steak insted, then stormed out of the office. The next time I saw that D/C was about five months later at the Crown Court trial of our skinhead villain.

The Crown Court story is quite interesting in itself. It was in Bristol Crown Court, in the presence of a High Court judge.

Our toerag skinhead villain had pleaded not guilty with his following defence and explanation of why he was hiding in that shed at 2am that morning. His alleged story was that on that particular night he found it difficult to sleep and so decided to go out jogging from his address in South Bristol, up across the downs in Clifton and then along Kellaway Avenue.

It was whilst jogging in Kellaway Avenue that he witnessed a group of men breaking into a shop and stealing boxes of something. He could not describe these men or make a suggestion as to what they were stealing, but one thing he did know was that he was frightened. He was really scared on two fronts:

1. This gang might spot him, realise that he'd be a witness and possibly do him some harm.
2. He readily admitted to having a criminal record (unusual to admit that to a jury), and thought that if the police saw him so close to a burglary they would assume that he was connected to the crime. What was he to do? Oh yes, he could hide and neither the criminals nor the police would know he was in the area. So that's what he did. He ran down some lanes, jumped over some garden walls and eventually found an outside toilet that was not locked. This is where he hid. He was very quiet. He intended to wait until first light and then walk home to

South Bristol. In fact, he would go on to tell the court how relieved he was when the police found him. It meant that he was safe and those nasty burglars could not harm him.

Well, it's as clear as the nose on your face. This poor little nocturnal jogger must be not guilty.

The trial continued for a day or two and then at the end, just prior to the jury retiring to consider their verdict, his honour the judge summed up the case for the benefit of the jury. Bearing in mind that a judge cannot say, "This man is guilty" or convict him; he can, however, in his summary direct the jury to consider certain facts of the case, and in this particular case the judge was keen to highlight the defence of jogging, and the associated running attire and footwear of those who jog.

The judge was brilliant. The exhibits were on a table in front of the jury. One exhibit was the pair of Dr Marten bovver boots. I don't know what size they were, but they were the high calf, twelve-hole variety in cherry red. When the judge began his direction to the jury he started to talk about how the defendant had decided to go jogging in the middle of the night, in a downpour, whilst wearing denim jeans and a jacket, and how the normal attire for such exercise was either shorts and a T-shirt or a tracksuit.

He then asked the court usher to bring over to his bench the pair of boots that the defendant was wearing at the time of his arrest. The judge then struggled to pick up the boots as he addressed the jury. Straining to hold the heavy boots aloft, the judge explained that from enquiries that he had made, the vast majority of joggers wore lightweight plimsolls whilst out jogging.

He looked directly at the jury and said, as he again struggled to hold these boots in the air for the jury to see, "Members of the jury, if you think that these boots are conducive to jogging then you may be inclined to believe the defendant. It's a matter for you."

The jury retired. An hour and fifteen minutes later, the verdict was guilty. Mr Skinhead was sent to prison for four years. This was one of my top five jobs that I had with Major. He located the prisoner and the stolen goods. Jobs like these do not come along very often.

Diary comment: *Major simply brilliant.*

20th March 1983
Park Street, Bristol
A Division

This was a simple stop check. Caught in possession of drugs.

21st March 1983
Video Shop, Cheltenham Road, Bristol
A Division

At about 3am on the 21st of March 1983 I attended an A1 (alarm activation) at a video rental shop in Cheltenham Road, Bristol. The actual video shop was on the first floor of this terraced building. I think the ground floor was a photocopier sundries company.

Upon my arrival I found a youth loitering nearby who I was not happy with at all. He had gloves and a screwdriver in his possession and his story just did not add up. I nicked him on suspected attempted burglary. It later transpired that he was in fact the lookout for the burglary. Upon looking at the front of the premises, there was no sign of a break-in, therefore we just sat tight and waited for the keyholder to arrive.

Upon the keyholder gaining entry for us, I went up the stairs and immediately saw that the very high ceiling was smashed in and there was debris all over the stairs and landing. Entry had been gained through the roof. The guy outside was the lookout, but where was Mr Burglar? Upon searching the small offices, which had been ransacked, Major located the intruder concealed behind a filing cabinet in a small office. This guy was not bitten – he was in such a tight, inaccessible spot that the barking, growling Major simply couldn't get to him.

We later found out that Mr Burglar could not find anything high enough to gain access to the damaged ceiling to get back out onto the roof and escape. He apparently had watched me and the dog arrive and then hid in trepidation, knowing that he couldn't escape.

Diary comment: *crafty crook.*

21st March 1983
Kingswood High Street, Bristol
E Division

Failing to stop after a road traffic accident; one person arrested for a positive breath test.

18th April 1983
Robinson Drive, Easton, Bristol
A Division

A youth was acting suspiciously near a house in Robinson Drive in the middle of the night. When stopped he had a selection of housebreaking implements on him. One youth was nicked for going equipped.

17th May 1983
Burglary at the Sportsman's Club, Eastville Stadium, Bristol

Once again we were on nights and we received a call to the Sportsman's Club, which is situated in the Old Eastville car park of what in those days was the home of Bristol Rovers.

Upon our arrival local units confirmed that the rear door had been forced, no one had gone in and the place was surrounded. The bad news was that the audible alarm was sounding, and that probably meant our villains had gone.

Despite the bells blaring away I did a quick search of the club just to make sure no intruders were still present. Major had a quick zoom around too and they had gone; however, not before both fruit machines and the cigarette machine had been forced open – obviously a fair bit of gear had been nicked.

As luck would have it the A Division lads had only secured the perimeter of the building. They had not strayed far out from the club, so a track might be possible. It was a dry night with just a slight breeze; it had rained earlier but not for a couple of hours. I put my tracking harness on Major and almost instantly his nose went to the ground and he began to sniff aggressively, sucking in air up his hooter faster than a Dyson vacuum. The benefit to me was that the tarmac surface of the car park was in a poor condition, and was broken up in quite a few places. This made it slightly easier for the scent disturbance to be retained a while longer.

I initially cast around just a short distance from the obvious exit point that the villains would have taken. It wasn't easy, but after a few minutes Major located a track on the broken surface and was off. The track did not go in the most direct way away from the club, as this would have taken the raiders into the light beams of the tall car park lamps. It went straight into the shadows and up to the chain-link fence that borders the gas plant at the rear of the Old Eastville Stadium. (A little note to those football fans who are reading this book: Bristol Rovers' nickname is 'The Gas' after the old coal gas works at the rear of the stadium.)

We then tracked all along the perimeter fence in the general direction of Muller Road. Major's tracking was pretty good; I reckon we were twenty or twenty-five minutes behind the bad guys. We skirted the stadium and then went up onto the old cinder pitches near to the greyhound kennels at the rear of Eastville. We were going on steadily, quite slowly in fact, as a semi-hard surface track tends to go. I think a couple of A Division lads were shadowing me about fifty yards back, not close enough to influence or interrupt the dog. A couple of times we obviously overshot as Major would stop, go in circles, retrace his steps and then be off again.

We were now coming out of Eastville near to Muller Road, but then we went off to the left and seemed to be skirting the old railway embankment, which ran parallel with Ingmire Road. We were then onto grass and mud and we seemed to perk up a bit. We continued in this grassy undergrowth, then all at once found ourselves in one of the old railway arches that honeycomb the old railway embankment. Major was ahead of me, some twenty feet in the dark, and I heard the clanging sound of metal on metal. Upon joining him I found that he had located a canvas haversack that had a jemmy, two hammers, some screwdrivers and two pairs of gloves inside it. This later transpired to have been abandoned by the offenders as they made good their escape; no doubt they would have returned later to recover their tools.

We then had to retrace our steps to the mouth of the railway archway and try yet again to relocate the villains' track. Major was doing his best on the far side of the archway when *wham!* He suddenly hit it off; we went up and over the embankment and down into the lane that runs along the rear of Ingmire Road. Along the lane it was quite muddy and wet. We continued for about fifty yards and he suddenly shot into somebody's rear garden. We went straight up to the rear door, which was locked. Upon shining my torch through the glass of the door I saw fresh muddy footprints on the kitchen floor. Trinity supervisory informed me the property was sealed front and rear, and upon officers knocking on the door and eventually entering they found two brothers and all of the stolen monies and goods from the Sportsman's Club.

Diary comment: *Terrific, brilliant job.* Even after thirty-two years I wholeheartedly agree. It was a great track by a great dog.

9th July 1983
The Day I Started a Riot and Nearly Got Ray Holmes and Myself Killed
J Division

As a copper, if there was one thing I hated it was yobs. Foul-mouthed young men or women who simply had no respect for anyone or anything.

The weekend of the 9th and 10th July was a mega yob weekend at Weston-super-Mare. Weston Borough Council had seen fit to grant a licence for a mod weekend. Now don't get me wrong, in the late 60s I was a bit of a mod myself, but not a yob mod. Over this weekend thousands of youngsters on motor scooters had invaded Weston from all over the south of England. I also think 80% of all the mods from Birmingham were in town.

To begin with, things weren't too bad, but as the day wore on the behaviour of a particular group of yobs became cause for concern. There were honestly well over a hundred of these idiots in a seafront bar just up opposite Knightstone. This bar, like many others, had a large frontage with tables and chairs, which under normal circumstances would be very pleasant for families to have a nice beer or two whilst sat in the sunshine. However, on this occasion this was not the case. The ever-increasing gang of morons were becoming drunker by the hour. Liberties were starting to be taken, and some coppers were turning a blind eye and bottling out, I'm sad to say.

Ray Holmes and I were double-crewed in a Bristol dog van. There were quite a few dogs on duty that day as trouble was anticipated. We were travelling along the seafront from the direction of the Grand Pier up towards Knightstone and the Marine Lake. Ray was driving, and we had Storm and Major with us. Both dogs had been barking non-stop and to be honest they were giving me a headache. We were about seventy to eighty yards away from a bar, I believe it was called Mr Smith's, where all these yobs were gathered, when I saw, to my horror, a beer mug lobbed up over the traffic and onto the road by someone in this crowd. It then smashed on the beachside promenade, showering pedestrians in glass. There were families with children and elderly folk being intimidated by these louts.

As we got closer (the traffic was heavy and very slow-moving) I saw another beer mug launched about fifty feet into the air. This too came crashing down, sending dangerous glass all across the promenade. This was, to me, like an Avon & Somerset scud missile attack. One thing that really upset me was that there was a passing police vehicle very near to this latest launch, but it did nothing, simply kept on driving. Then to my horror again, as we drew level with Mr Smith's I saw a yob in a very distinctive yellow top lob yet another beer mug up in the air over the traffic and onto the opposite promenade. The yobs were laughing and swearing, intimidating everyone in sight.

Now I did not lose sight of Matey Boy in his yellow top. I told Ray to turn the van around and stop outside Mr Smith's. I had eyeball contact with Mr Yellow Top, and as I got out of the van I was greeted with lots of whistles, jeers, pig snorting sounds and the old favourite,

The Police Take the Piss tune (I'm sure you know what I mean). I called out to Yellow Top to come over as I wanted a word with him. I was stood by my wide-open van door. Yellow Top sauntered slowly over towards me, constantly playing to the crowd who were lapping it up and taking the piss big time. He felt safe; he had over a hundred mates around him and there were just two coppers.

He grinned as he finally got to me and said, "What do you want, Mr Plod?", and everyone laughed and jeered. The row was deafening as these yobs chanted this kid's nickname.

I said, "Come a bit closer, I can't hear with all of this noise." He came a bit closer and I positioned myself to the right of the open passenger door. I gently put my arm on his shoulder and said, "You're an arsehole."

He said, "What?", and with that I shoved him into the van and screamed, "You're nicked! You are not obliged to say anthing etc…" He fell into the van and I quickly followed, slamming the door behind me. I screamed at Ray to "Go! Go! Go!", but Yellow Top was sat on the handbrake. We were going nowhere!

Suddenly the world erupted! Our van windows were wide open because it was very hot. *Bang! Crash! Bang! Wallop! Smash! Bang!* Dozens of beer glasses, ashtrays, chairs, tables, in fact everything and anything hit the van. It was very noisy and frightening. One funny thing did happen. A beer mug came sailing in through the open window, just missing me, just missing Yellow Top, just missing Ray and then out of Ray's window!

It was really scary. Yellow Top was no longer the hard man; he was crying, "Get us out of here." Our van took a hell of a bashing; it was trashed. This was a war zone.

Ray managed to get his hand through Yellow Top's legs to release the handbrake and we were off. It was like *Black Hawk Down* and *A Bridge Too Far* all rolled into one.

Back at Weston nick, Yellow Top was processed, stayed in and went to court on the Monday. A mini riot took place at Mr Smith's, for which Ray and I later received suitable advice.

Nothing like a nice, peaceful visit to the seaside!

Diary comment: *Very hairy time.*

20th July 1983
Crew's Hole Road, St George, Bristol
D Division

This was a simple vehicle stop check. Two nasty young criminals, one of whom later became 'public enemy number one'.

The criminal in question had £300 cash in his sock. Major's aggressive presence certainly kept both of them quiet. Burglary tools were found in the car (jemmies, balaclavas and hammers). They were nasty people even at this early age.

22nd July 1983
Longcross, Lawrence Weston, Bristol
C Division

A youth was reported trying to steal a motorcar. He was located in a nearby street trying to break into another car.

19th August 1983
Temple Way, City Centre, Bristol
A Division

This was a road traffic unit. PC Dave Phillips (one of Major's bite victims) was chasing a suspected stolen motorcycle around the A Division. This ended when the motorbike crashed in Temple Way. The rider escaped injury and ran off and was lost to sight.

We turned up and Major located the offender hiding in bushes on wasteland. The offender received a minor nip on his bum for his trouble.

I arrested him. It was a guilty plea.

22nd August 1983
Wyck Beck Road Garage, Passage Road, Henbury, Bristol
C Division

On nights again. It was around 1am and four youths had broken into the petrol station in Wyck Beck Road. A fair amount of property had been stolen, including a bank bag and all of the day's cash takings. Upon the arrival of the first C Division unit four youths were seen to run off from within the attacked premises.

Three young men were detained within the first hundred yards. However, one youth was lost to sight as he ran into the Passage Road area. I was in Passage Road within two minutes and I saw a youth answering the offender's description walking in Passage Road.

I basically pulled up alongside him, with Major hanging out of my van window spitting fire. I requested him to stop, which thankfully for him and me, he did. He was out of breath and sweating. He was nicked on suspicion of burglary and conveyed in custody to Southmead Police Station. He had absolutely nothing in his possession.

After liaising with C Division units I decided to harness Major up and we backtracked from where I had stopped Matey Boy to the petrol station in Wyck Beck Road.

What was amazing was that towards the end of the track, about two hundred yards from the garage, Major stopped. He thrust his head into a hedge and after about twenty seconds appeared with the stolen bank bag and money in his mouth. Obviously my offender had quickly shoved the bag into the hedge as the other three were being nicked. A great job!

Diary comment: *A nice little job.*

23rd August 1983
Priory Avenue, Henleaze, Bristol
C Division

A middle-aged man was disturbed while committing a burglary at a dwelling in Henleaze, Bristol. He was chased by the occupier out into the street and lost to sight. PD Major found the offender in the nearby garden. He was detained.

This guy was in fact an escapee from Dartmoor prison.

9th November 1983
Ambleside Avenue, Southmead, Bristol
C Division

Windows were smashed on a house in Ambleside Avenue in the middle of the night. Whilst searching the area PD Major located the offender concealed behind a wall in Wigton Crescent.

It was a simple job and a lovely indication by the dog.

31st December 1983
Hillfields, Fishponds, Bristol
D Division

S/V was chased by another dog handler (Neil Barnes). It was abandoned and Neil nicked two youths. I arrested a third offender climbing over the wall of the Chequers pub in Ingleside Road.

4th January 1984
Kelston Road, Henleaze, Bristol
C Division

Three youths were disturbed syphoning petrol from a car in Henleaze. When confronted by a very aggressive Major they decided to surrender and plead guilty.

6th January 1984
Burglary at Gardner Haskins Superstore, Broad Plain, Bristol
A Division
Danny Boy's Regret

If only this thoroughly nasty and obnoxious Irish chap had surrendered like his burglar accomplice, then he would have saved himself a lot of pain and suffering, plus a few days' stay in the Bristol Royal Infirmary.

It was well after 2am on the 6th January 1984. It was cold but I don't think we had had much snow up until then. We had received an A1 (alarm activation) call to the Gardner Haskins Superstore in Broad Plain, Bristol. A road traffic car and I arrived simultaneously in Broad Plain, just in time to see two burglars very dangerously climbing out of a huge smashed plate glass window of the store. It transpired that these were two Irish fellas from the itinerant travelling community. The first guy out of the window ran off down the road shouting out profanities as he went. Major said hello to the second gent, who promptly surrendered to the traffic boys.

Now 'Danny Boy' was about eighty yards ahead of me. I shouted that I would release the dog if he didn't stop. He yelled back, "F*** you and your dog", and climbed over the six-foot wall that gave access to the old Redifussion TV rental company vehicle yard, and was lost to sight – but not for long.

The yard was totally enclosed and secure. Danny Boy had sealed his own fate – he was going nowhere.

The first bit of bad news was that although it was a six-foot climb to get up, it was more like a ten or twelve-foot drop down into the yard. The yard itself was predominately full of Rediffusion vans of varying types and sizes. To the left of the compound was a single-storey portacabin that acted as the transport office for Rediffusion, and about ten feet from the portacabin was the metal fire escape that was part of the Gardner Haskins building they had just burgled. This fire escape was on the five storey-high wall of Gardner's that formed the left-hand perimeter of the Rediffusion yard.

With the first Irishman safely cuffed and in the back of the traffic car, I went with Major to the bit of the wall where Danny Boy had climbed over. Hindsight is a great thing because on reflection I should have had a look over the wall to see what I was putting Major into, but I didn't. The adrenaline was pumping; Major was up for it, growling, snorting and raring to go. I gave the command "up" and my dog was up and over the wall in a flash. I climbed the wall and straddled it, surveying the canvas below me.

Oh dear! Poor old Major – he had landed in a heap twelve feet below me, and I am sure that he was not a happy bunny.

On glancing over I could see Danny Boy, who was now limping quite badly; I can only assume he also had a dodgy landing the other side of Becher's Brook. He was heading for the metal fire escape, and upon seeing me he screamed out, "You're all a bunch of f*****g c***s!" I then saw him climb the fire escape until he was level with the roof of the portacabin. He climbed onto the handrail of the escape and then leapt about nine or ten feet over onto the roof of the portacabin. I was quite impressed, but I did think, what on earth is he doing? My attention returned to Major, who was just getting to his feet, having a good shake and basically dusting himself down for the main course.

He had caught sight of Danny Boy scampering up the fire escape and noted how he had courageously leapt across onto the portacabin roof. With his sat nav duly tuned in, Major was off like an Exocet missile.

This is honestly what occurred. What made Major so unique was that he acted upon impulse by himself. Really I think he only needed me to feed him once a day and do his washing and ironing.

As Major tore across the ground he was making quite terrifying snarling and growling noises. He was quite literally hunting, and his prey was in full view. Now, whilst Major was running over in his general direction, Danny Boy obviously felt quite safe and confident that his current position was unassailable. He felt so confident that he was shouting profanities to Major like, "Send your f*****g dog, I will kill him. F*** you, you c***."

I was now gingerly negotiating my descent down the wall into the yard. I firmly believe that my landing was much softer and more acceptable than either Major's or Danny Boy's. I landed just in time to see Major reach the fire escape. In an instant he was jumping the metal steps at a considerable speed.

Danny Boy's attitude suddenly changed, and on seeing the fast-approaching Major his self-preservation mode began to take over. He was scampering around the roof, frantically looking for anything to defend himself with in the unlikely event that this loony dog should somehow gain access to the portacabin roof.

With panic in his eyes, Danny Boy at last found an implement to repel Major if required: a long-handled snow board clearer. This was what was used to push the snow into piles in the winter from around the vans in the yard. It was a four-foot-long wooden handle with a three-by-two-foot board at the end. For clearing snow, probably 10/10; for repelling Major in full flight, 0/10.

A little bit of the colour returned to Danny Boy's cheeks. A tiny bit of confidence returned; he even managed to shout, "Come on, you c***" as he brandished the snow board in defiance.

What I witnessed next was unbelievable! Major, who was now in full flight up the fire escape, got to the landing that was level with the portacabin roof and without breaking stride, simply leapt the three-foot railing, cleared the ten-foot gap and landed on the portacabin roof. On my life, this happened – no input from me whatsoever.

Danny Boy's bravado seemed to drain away from him. Armed with his snow board, he managed to fend Major off for a little while. However, with every attack Major was dismantling Danny's snow board. It was just like a *Tom & Jerry* cartoon where you just know how it's going to end.

I was now over at the fire escape and starting to climb the stairs. I could see onto the roof, and the final throes of Danny Boy's pathetic resistance. His last piece of board was bitten off and spat out by Major, who was primed for the kill.

Danny Boy, upon seeing me, screamed out, "OK, boss, I give up, no problem," as he threw the last eighteen inches of handle down and raised his hands in surrender.

Well, there I was, ten feet away over on the fire escape. I might as well have been on the moon. I could have shouted, "Major, leave! Major, no! Major, down!" or I could have spoken to him in Chinese, Russian or Punjabi – all would have been to no avail. The end result was that Danny Boy was going to pay for his indiscretions…and he did, via the Bristol Royal Infirmary.

Even today, I think of how Major leapt across from that fire escape onto the portacabin of his own accord; it simply was amazing.

Diary comment: *Unbelievable.*

3rd March 1984
Clifton College, Guthrie Road, Clifton, Bristol
C Division

Three suspect youths were arrested wearing balaclavas in the grounds of Clifton College, in the middle of the night. Burglary tools were found in their possession.

3rd March 1984
Co-op Shirehampton, Bristol
C Division

This was a smash-and-grab. One offender was found in the graveyard with stolen spirits (no pun intended) and cigarettes.

29th March 1984
Greenlands Road, Henbury Road, Bristol
C Division

A stolen vehicle was abandoned and one offender ran off. PD Major tracked them to the offender's house. It was only about a hundred yards.

30th March 1984
Coldharbour Road, Redland, Bristol
C Division

A positive breath test.

25th May 1984
Redland Green Tennis Club, Redland, Bristol

During the night I attended a confirmed burglary at the Redland Tennis Club, Redland, Bristol.

As seemed to be the case with these burglaries, the fruit machines were the usual targets. On this occasion one gaming machine had been broken into and a considerable number of 50p pieces had been stolen.

Major located a track, and whilst tracking we firstly found £200 in 50p pieces and then a suspected burglar nearby who was certainly under the influence of drink.

Arrested and admitted offence.

28th May 1984
Epworth Road, Henbury, Bristol
C Division

A few nights prior to this job we had experienced a number of smash-and-grab raids at chemists in the north of Bristol. We had two suspects who we knew were using a stolen motorcycle as part of the raids on these chemists' shops. The villains were stealing predominately perfumes.

On the night of 28th May a stolen car that had been involved in a ram raid was chased and lost in the Passage Road area of Bristol. Within five minutes it was located, abandoned in Epworth Road, Henbury. The car had sustained damage to the rear where it had been reversed through a chemist's window, and stolen goods, including perfumes, were still in the car. When it was found the occupants had made off.

Upon my arrival at the scene, I harnessed PD Major and within minutes he had located a track. We then tracked on a hard surface, plus the occasional stretch of grass for over half a mile to the address of one of the suspects.

Stolen property was located in a shed at this property. Entry was gained and two known criminals who were our main suspects were arrested. Two stolen crash helmets were found in the garden of this address.

Diary comment: *Bloody good track, very pleased.*

3rd June 1984
Sports Pavilion, Clanage Road, Bower Ashton, Bristol
B Division

There was a report of noise coming from the sports pavilion on a Sunday afternoon. I attended with PS Instone. Three were arrested for attempted theft of copper pipe.

21st July 1984
Pembroke Road, Clifton, Bristol
C Division

This job involved three yobs in a stolen car; all well-known criminals and bang at it – active villains.

They were in a stolen Ford Escort van and were out and about committing crime. The driver was also a disqualified driver. The van stopped in Pembroke Road, Clifton, Bristol. All three were nicked without incident.

Diary comment: *Nice little pick-up.*

22nd July 1984
Watkins Court, Westbury-on-Trym, Bristol
C Division

Three youths ran off upon seeing me. They were chased and I detained two. One got away. On returning to where I originally saw them, I discovered a number of cars that had been broken into.

Diary comment: *A very neat, lucky little job.*

Before I get on to telling you a few of my favourite Major stories, I think I should explain just a little about a weekly potential public order situation that occurred in Bristol, August till May every year. This nine-monthly event also happens in lots of cities up and down the country, but perhaps even more so in the late 70s and 80s. This event being football duty.

Bristol has two professional football clubs: Bristol City FC, who play in red and whose home is Ashton Gate, and Bristol Rovers FC, who play in blue and whose home ground at this time was Eastville Stadium in Bristol.

The City have generally been the more successful club, and currently play in the football championship. The Rovers, who over the years have been less successful, are currently in Division 2. (Just been promoted back up to Division 1 at the time of writing this. UP THE GAS!)

Back in 1976 the City won promotion to the old first division (now the premier league), and remained there for four years until they were relegated in 1980. From 1975 till 1981 the Rovers were in the old second division (now the first division).

Upon joining the dog section in 1978 I was fortunate enough to perform duties at Ashton Gate for two and a half years whilst the City were still in the top division. This meant that for over two seasons I got to see the likes of Man United, Liverpool, Chelsea, Spurs, West Ham, Leeds and many more top clubs.

It also meant that every City home game was a seventeen thousand plus sell-out, with the potential for public disorder. Unfortunately, these were the days of the football hooligan, and the notorious Chelsea Head Hunters and the West Ham Inter City Firm were just two of the violent gangs that posed quite serious problems.

Every City home game was like a military operation, and dogs and horses were two of the tools which were available to the police commanders to help combat any trouble. These matches were both exciting and challenging.

Football at Eastville with the Rovers could be challenging depending on the opponents (Cardiff City, for example). One thing that we did tend to get involved with at both grounds was the escorting of visiting fans from either Temple Meads Railway Station to Ashton Gate (about two and a half miles), or the much shorter quarter-mile route from Stapleton Road Station to Eastville.

These escorts involved anything up to five hundred visiting fans being herded in a convoy along the main roads to the stadiums, flanked by uniform officers on foot with dogs and horses scattered along the length of the convoys. Task force vans and police motorcyclists would also make up the convoy.

Bearing in mind these happy away day supporters were normally shouting and chanting loud, provocative songs in an attempt to wind up any locals, the general atmosphere was normally buzzing. Major needed no excuse to get wound up, so this excess noise merely put him in overdrive. He really was hard work on a football convoy. He would want to bite anyone in sight, and this meant that I always had him on the shortest lead possible. I used to have the index finger of my left hand looped through the link of his chain closest to his neck, which in turn meant that he was bouncing off my thigh for the duration of the escort. Sometimes in sheer frustration he would turn his head and nip me on the knee, as if to say, "Let me at 'em", and both of my uniform trouser legs had lots of tiny snags in them where Major had nipped me.

Amazingly enough I had very few bites at football, I believe because firstly Major was on a very short lead at all times, and also because he was so outwardly aggressive that fans and police alike always gave us a wide berth, and tended to avoid us at all costs.

However, a couple of incidents stick out in my mind concerning football duties. Both were at Ashton Gate. There was the match against a Welsh team, when the away fans attacked and destroyed the turnstiles near to the Duckmoor Road end. Then there was the hand-to-hand fighting against a South London club's fans, who had allegedly raided every snooker hall in South London prior to the game and stolen all of the snooker balls, which they then used as ammunition against the Bristol City fans and us. I think this was also game where one of our unattended dog vans was turned upon its roof by this club's hooligan element.

I cannot finish this little tale without singing the praises of Alan Jobbins and Gerry Haskey, the two mounted sergeants who with their cavalry colleagues on many occasions came galloping to my and many a dog handler's rescue on days gone by in Ashton Park.

Eventful days for sure, but with the City's subsequent relegations and the general decline in football violence things quietened down considerably.

FAVOURITE MAJOR STORIES

The date is early in 1980. I had only had Major for a few months; I was probably in my second or third set of nights after finishing my course with him.

I was now covering the Central & Trinity Road A Division. What I found quite difficult was coming to terms with the fact that I now had a police dog that looked and sounded in all aspects like a police dog. Bearing in mind that for the previous year I had worked with my little, pretty bitch Dena, who was truthfully no great shakes, the change to me was massive. It was all about building a reputation for myself and my new dog. I fully appreciated that my reputation with Dena was not very impressive at all.

I do recall one night with Dena when we were in the Berkeley Square/Brandon Hill area. A youth had been disturbed breaking into cars. He was chased by a bobby on foot patrol in Park Street, but had been lost to sight on the approach to Brandon Hill.

Dena was off the lead and was very gingerly searching in amongst the parked cars. Unknown to me, as we made our way up to the back entrance of the car park, a road traffic sergeant (Paul Waters) was approaching this same car park entrance from the Brandon Hill direction.

What happened next would not have been out of place in a *Carry On* film. Remember that Dena did not like the dark? Well, both Dena and Sgt Waters turned the corner of the wall at the same time. It was a calamity as Sgt Waters screamed, "Oh shit!" and nearly fainted. Dena was frightened to death, yelped and ran off with her tail between her legs, and was lost to sight. It took me a good few minutes to find Dena, who was by this time fifty yards away at the other side of Berkeley Square.

The point in telling this story is to illustrate to my readers that my previous police dog was a bit of a liability, to say the least. My new dog Major was not going to be a wimp! He was already shaping up nicely, and I would often get the local A Division boys to gee him up when he was in the van. The last thing you wanted was people approaching your van and your dog not reacting.

Now would be a good time to explain that every month you were rostered two or three official training days. Also, every year you would have a two-week training refresher course. Having said all that, training was an ongoing affair throughout your dog's life. Quite often you would take a leather bite sleeve out with you on nights, meet up with the handler from an adjoining division and do some street criminal work. This was as a rule done after 4am when things were quietening down.

One thing that I got the A Division boys to help me with were dog chases from the van. By this I mean that I would encourage Major to exit the van quickly and chase after a suspect.

I mentioned earlier that you should never assume that your dog has seen what you have seen. Here's why:

1. Regarding incidents that occur whilst your dog is out with you on foot on its lead, please bear in mind that the average six-foot copper has his eye level at about 5'6". A German Shepherd dog's eye level is probably somewhere between two feet and 2'6" from ground level. Consequently, what you see happening over a three-foot wall, or what happens on a brow of a hill or lane, may not necessarily have been seen by your dog.

2. As for incidents that occur whilst your dog is in your van, I am putting my head on the block here, but if you keep your dog secure in the rear cage of your dog van then the chances of him

responding instantly to an incident that happens in front of you are remote. If something occurs, once you've stopped you have to get out of the van, run around to open the van's back door; then open the cage doors and get your dog out. Vital seconds are lost, and that criminal who is running away has been lost to sight and your dog hasn't a clue what is happening or what is expected of him.

Conversely, I normally had Major's cage door open (he was always in the cage behind the front seat passenger). This meant he was loose, taking in the views and situations just like me. In addition, he was also trained to leap out of the passenger window, but more likely follow me out of my door as I exited the van. This tactic saved vital seconds and meant Major was fully aware of whom to pursue if necessary.

This has been quite a long and expansive explanation of the next story; however, I felt I had to explain what I was doing and why.

*

Back to the night in question, and the location was Broadmead. It was quiet and I don't quite know how a cadet was on nights, but he was (it must have been his street attachments prior to going away to DTC).

I somehow persuaded this young lad to gee Major up and then run the fifty or sixty yards to the red phone box by Virgin Records and hide in that said telephone box. The plan was for me not to release Major until this lad was easily within reach of the phone box and sanctuary.

Well, all went according to plan. The cadet came up to the van, geed up Major, who went ballistic, and then ran off towards the phone box. Major, on seeing the guy run off, went mad, barking and growling with dog spit flying everywhere in the van.

When I was sure that the guy was safe I reached over and opened the passenger door and Major was off. By the time I got out and was running, Major was two thirds of the way there and my cadet was in the phone box. To my horror, when I looked at the telephone kiosk I could see that the door was still closing very, very slowly. In fact, it did close about a nanosecond before Major could get his snout into the opening.

My goodness me, that cadet was pulling on the door in sheer panic; his face was white. I think it was one of those slow-closing mechanisms where the more you tried to pull, the slower it closed. That boy had aged about forty years! Major was going loopy; he was snapping and snarling quite aggressively.

Hindsight is a great thing, and as I write this I am thinking, what if that lad had tripped or stumbled and not made it to the phone box? The consequences do not bear thinking about, and the health and safety implications are horrendous!

My volunteer on that night – Phil Petela, Cadet 36, latterly PS 1345 and now, thankfully, retired and bar – kindly responded to my appeal for recollections and anecdotes. His version of events is below:

> I saw the little piece in the Bristol NARPO news and was instantly reminded of the 'race' you talked me into in 1980 in Broadmead between me and Major. I had a head start to get

to a phone box just along by what was then Virgin Records. As a young, fit cadet I thought, no problem. Well, I beat the dog to the phone box, no problem. What I hadn't taken into account was the leather door hinges that only allowed the flipping door to close very slowly. Major was bearing down, the door was creaking shut and all I had for protection was a copy of the Yellow Pages! Thankfully by the time Major reached the phone box the door was closed too far for him to get his nose in. I have never raced another dog again. I still tell people about it now.

The Phantom Bite
Penn Street, Broadmead, Bristol
A Division, 1983

This was a job, an attack and a dog bite that was never officially recorded. It was about 1.30am on a night tour and I was slowly chugging in first gear with my lights off along Penn Street in Bristol. Major, as normal, was out of the cage, stood at my side with his head resting upon my shoulder; he was constantly scanning the horizon for any activity and any possible targets.

As we progressed along Penn Street my attention was drawn to the doorway of the C&A clothing store. I had seen a head pop back and forth a couple of times; Major had spotted it too and was beginning to growl and curl his lip. My first thought was that someone was screwing the place. I accelerated now with lights on, and Major went into 'pre-attack mode'. Almost immediately the figure of a young man, about seventeen or eighteen years old, ran out from the doorway and was on his toes down Penn Street towards Broad Weir.

I stopped the van, shouted a challenge and then let Major leap out of the passenger window. He had clocked him immediately and was chasing after him like a flash. Matey Boy suddenly turned left into a small courtyard that led out onto Bond Street, and was lost to sight, shortly followed by Major, who was also lost to sight.

I drove into the courtyard, stopped the van and – nothing! Five seconds later I heard the familiar scream of agony coming from behind a large waste skip in the courtyard. I closed in, released the lad from Major's grip and saw that his leg had a couple of puncture wounds.

In all the rush and confusion, I had not had time to put in a radio call to A Division – just as well, as it happens. The reason being that this lad was the son of a local licensee, who was a good friend to the bobbies at Central. There was no real criminal offence as he was simply having a piss in the shop doorway as I drove by. Upon seeing the police vehicle, he panicked and ran off.

I quietly arranged for another officer to contact the lad's father and they were reunited at the BRI. The lad's clean record was still intact, a painful lesson had been learned and his dad was more pro-police than ever!

The Smell!
Temple Back, Just Down From the Avon Fire Brigade HQ

A short, amusing little story, with believe it or not, no bites, no aggression and no prisoners! However, the memory lingers with me to this day, thirty-five years on!

The location was the large piece of wasteland in Temple Back, where the DAS building was built. Back in the early 1980s this was just a bombsite awaiting redevelopment. This grassy site was about eighty yards wide by twenty-five deep, and it backed onto the Floating Harbour. For an A Division dog handler it was a great place for letting your dog have a pee. Now, one thing I have to explain to you, if you didn't already know, is that all dogs are basically predatory hunters. I believe that all dogs have originated from the wolf. In the wild when it is hunting its prey, a wild dog would do a couple of things:

1. Try to approach its prey from a downwind position. In doing so, the dog's own scent would not be blown in the direction of the prey, and he would hopefully remain undetected for as long as possible.
2. The predator (dog) would mask his own scent by rolling in other animals' faeces or by rolling in carrion or decomposing flesh.

Back to the story in question. It was about 2am on a night shift and I was giving Major a run at this particular site. I had released him from the van with the command to "be quick" – which means 'have a dump'. With training you could get your dogs to crap on command. It's always a good idea to allow your dog a dump in case they have to go in and search a building. Nothing worse than searching somewhere and your dog leaving a steaming parcel on someone's floor! Well, off he went into the depths of the bombsite and was lost to sight amongst all the weeds and vegetation in the darkness. After five minutes I called him, with no response. I called him again and again, but nothing. In the end I had no option but to venture out into the undergrowth and find him. I spent a good few minutes calling his name and searching, but to no avail.

I eventually honed in on some nuzzly, wriggly noises. Yes, it was Major and he was away with the fairies! I caught him laid on his back and he was wriggling and shuffling his body in a combination of fox shit and the maggot-infested carcass of a dead chicken. For those of you who do not know what fox shit smells like, I can honestly say it is as bad as a dead rat.

It is one million per cent disgusting!

The swine of a dog that was Major was very reluctant to leave his stench pit. I had a devil of a job putting his choke chain on and dragging him away from the putrid, smelly mass. The smell. THE SMELL. It was of horrendous proportions! I simply had no option but to go back to Bower and set about shampooing him and cleaning him up. Plus I'd have to clean the van (I was thinking of the poor sod who had to use it the next morning). I was also very paranoid about putting this pungent beast into my own car.

I will not prolong the cleaning story, but just to say it took the next three hours and my name was mud on the section for weeks. That smell stayed around for about six weeks and no one let me forget it.

For once you could say, "his smell was worse than his bite" – and that was saying something!

Traffic Officer So Very Nearly Lost an Eye

I am not sure of the year, possibly 1983. The location was Bristol city centre. It was most likely on a Friday or Saturday night. I cannot recall the reason why, but there was large-scale crowd disorder. Yobs were fighting with police officers all across the city centre. The reason I know this was large-scale disorder is because normally traffic officers would not get involved with low-level divisional punch-ups. However, when the chips were down it would have been a case of 'all hands to the pumps'.

On this particular night I can recall being on the City Centre with Major. We were out of the van dispersing groups of disorderly youths. I had Major on a short lead and he was very effective at dispersing crowds. Believe me, when Major was on song, up on his back legs spitting fire – he truly was a formidable sight. No one in their right mind would hang around when the possibility of being bitten by old iron-jaws was in the offering.

I recall my attention had been drawn to a friend of mine, a traffic officer with some reputation himself. I firstly noticed his white top peaked cap, which was on the ground as he was being kicked in the body and face by a particularly nasty yob. The officer was on the ground trying to defend himself, and he had just succeeded in grabbing hold of this yob's leg, which at least meant he wasn't getting a kicking anymore.

Having cleared sufficient space to manoeuvre, I decided to approach this said yob and introduce him to some Major justice. The officer was still desperately hanging on to his leg, and as I closed in with Major, carefully aiming at the yob's leg, disaster struck. At the very last moment, the yob, on seeing the approaching dog, suddenly grabbed the officer's hair and swung his face around whilst lifting him slightly with his leg into the path of Major.

I tried to check Major's attack, pulling frantically on his lead to try and avoid contact with the officer's face. There was a very quick snap of Major's jaws and suddenly the yob was off and the officer was injured.

I don't recall what happened to the yob, but the poor officer had been bitten on his eyelid/eyebrow and required a couple of stitches up at the BRI hospital.

This was so close to being a terrible tragedy of gigantic proportions. Thank goodness there were no hard feelings from this officer, but this just added to the list of police who had been injured by Major.

The Night We Nicked a Rugby Team

It was a Saturday night in 1982. I was the dog handler covering Bristol's A Division. This was the centre of the South West's largest city, and it was extremely busy. One of the city's most popular attractions was the German Bierkeller in All Saints Lane, just off Fairfax Street. This venue was always very busy, with both local Bristolians and coachloads of visitors. These coach parties would come from as far away as Taunton, Swindon, Gloucester and South Wales.

Unfortunately, due to the large number of people who frequented this establishment, plus the strong steins of German beer sold, there was always the distinct possibility of trouble.

Our night shifts ran from 11pm through until 6am. Usually on Saturday nights it was not just the A Division dog who positioned himself near to this venue. Our dog sergeant, Vernon Essex, was as a rule also nearby, and on this Saturday the C Division handler, Mike Shepherd, was also in the vicinity. I recall that during the changeover at Bower Ashton the late turn A Division handler had commented that town was very busy indeed, and that the area around All Saints Lane was popping, especially by the Bierkeller.

By 11.30pm I was in All Saints Lane with officers from Central. I was out of my van standing with a group of A Division lads when we were suddenly called into the now heaving German beer club to a disturbance at the top of the entrance stairs.

I can remember seeing one young man laid out cold on the pool table. I think an ambulance was called and small skirmishes were happening at various points in the Bierkeller. One large group of guys who seemed intent on causing trouble were a coachload of rugby players from the Gloucester area. Around this time, I was joined by Sgt Essex and Mike Shepherd. All three dog vans were parked outside in All Saints Lane, and believe me, they were rocking.

Vernon's dog Sacha was very tasty and Mike's dog Rebel was also a mature, hard dog. Those two and Major made our dog team that night truly formidable.

The Central inspector correctly identified that the coachload of Gloucester boys were without doubt the obvious catalyst for serious crowd disorder. A group of about fifty men (rugby players are no strangers to a bit of violence either) was too large a group to allow them the freedom of the city. The rugby organiser was read the riot act and told to get his boys on the coach and to get out of town.

The coach was eventually loaded up and we all thought our problems were about to drive off back up the M5. The coach, fully loaded, drove off down All Saints Lane, then around and down Fairfax Street. Then suddenly a shout for assistance went up, and all hell broke loose. As Vernon, Mike and I arrived at the coach I could see A Division officers were trying to board the coach, and were being assaulted.

I could see an A Division sergeant was having difficulty on the steps of the coach. I immediately went to his aid with Major on a very short lead. As I climbed the steps onto the coach a yobbo who was stood at the top of the steps kicked out and booted Major in the head. This was a silly mistake as Major instantly shook off the effects of the kick and bit this yob very aggressively in the leg. Suddenly a well-meaning PC (Phil Hutchings) came forward in an effort to take this person into custody. He climbed up the stairs and in doing so brushed against Major's flank. Again, in an instant, Major released the yob and promptly attacked the PC who was brushing past him. Unfortunately, he bit PC Hutchings quite badly. There was utter chaos, with fights going on everywhere.

Order was finally restored when Sgt Essex and Mike Shepherd and their dogs boarded the coach via the rear emergency door. I remained at the top of the stairs at the front. Eventually we arrested the entire coach party and the driver drove to the side entrance of Old

Bridewell where they were escorted by dogs into the cells.

Below is an email from retired PC Phil Hutchings entitled *Love bite by Major (near loss of the family jewels)*:

In about 1982, as usual on a Friday or Saturday night, we used to have a sergeant and about six officers outside the Bierkeller in All Saints Lane, Bristol city centre.

On this particular night there was trouble (as normal) inside and then outside the club, involving a coachload of rugby players from Gloucestershire. We eventually got them aboard the coach and the driver drove around the corner into Fairfax Street, where it stopped. Clearly the driver had problems on board, and as we gathered around the coach I went to the front, near to the door. It opened and I saw a couple of men kicking out at PS Keith Nuttal (recently deceased). I moved forward to help him, and as I did so he moved backwards as he knew that you and Major were approaching. I could not see this. As he moved, Major duly bit me on my upper right thigh (very near to the family jewels) and he didn't let go! I was in agony as he had punctured my large right thigh muscle.

Well, he let go, I reeled away in pain and found it very difficult to walk. The coach was escorted to the side entrance of Old Bridewell where they were all arrested. I was then taken to the Bristol Royal where I was treated. The bite was oval in shape and about ten inches long; purple, red and other colours with two large puncture wounds in my thigh muscle. Two of my colleagues, Gerry Clarke (acting PS and a good friend) and Kev Penhale, arrived to check on my welfare and have a giggle, especially as I had pink boxer shorts on. They didn't laugh after they saw the wound.

I think we weren't into two rest days and duly I returned to work. Funnily enough, on the day I returned to work you walked into the report-writing room with the dog. I was very close to needing a change of underwear. You also got me to stroke the dog! Cheers Pete!

Two Little Jobs With Major Where No One Was Bitten

What is quite funny about these two jobs is that they both occurred within about five doors of each other on the main A38 heading north out of Bristol.

The Massage Parlour Shit Job

This incident occurred in the winter of 1982. At the time we didn't have specialist explosive or drug dogs, so our general purpose dogs were also trained for drugs or explosives. Major was one such dog that was trained to locate explosives.

At around 2am on this day I responded to a bomb call at this particular massage premises. Now to my knowledge the IRA have never considered massage parlours to have any political, military or commercial relevance, so why an anonymous call saying there's a bomb in the massage parlour would carry so much credence, I do not know!

The officers initially attending the call ascertained that two disgruntled squaddies had been kicked out of this same massage parlour only a few hours earlier after behaving inappropriately. I cynically thought to myself that these two incidents might be related.

The duty inspector explained to me the ridiculous nature of the call, and that the target property had to be cleared of potential explosives.

I have a theory that the two offender squaddies were probably sat in their car nearby watching the girls and paying customers, having no option but to evacuate the massage parlour out into the dark, cold night, resulting in a loss of revenue to the establishment.

Well, the place was deserted and in we went to carry out our search. In spite of the absurd venue, the task had to be taken seriously. I for one did not want to be the police officer that missed an IED (Improvised Explosive Device) in a massage parlour.

One minor thought I had was that the two squaddies did have slightly more potential access to explosives than Mr Joe Public, and was there a remote possibility that they could have planted a bomb.

The place was searched with a negative result. However, a little incident did take place. I should explain that the place was 'minging'.

It had a conglomeration of about six tatty massage rooms, each of which had a massage table of sorts, a fan and a cheap shower cubicle and tray. The rooms were horrible, believe me. The plugholes of the shower trays were particularly scary and unpleasant. There were enough pubic hairs in and around these shower trays to have made a six-foot-square Afghan rug. There were stains and blotches on the horrible carpets, dozens of empty shampoo and body wash bottles and a fair supply of empty Durex packets.

When I came to the second floor, Major showed positive interest in a loose hardboard wall panel. I could not believe he was showing interest in this portion of wall, which when eased out led to a void space, behind which were the eaves of the roof. He was keen to go in and have a mooch around, and so he did (I think in hindsight it was either a rat or a cat he had smelt). This void was virtually inaccessible to a guy my size, but hey! He was the hound with the nose, not me.

He was gone about thirty seconds, and to be honest I was afraid that he might fall through the ceiling, but worse was to follow. Bearing in mind he was out of sight, I could hear him snorting and sniffing when all at once I heard, to my horror, one huge, squelchy dog fart and then the sound of liquid gastroenteritis oozing from Major's bottom. The smell was unimaginable. It stank like a dozen dead rats. He quickly exited this roof space with a look on his face which said, "I needed that!"

There was no way I could even access this space, so I quickly pushed the hardboard panel back in place and tapped in the securing panel pins with my truncheon.

This was definitely one of Bristol's tourist hot spots that needed to be removed from the local tour guide.

Mind Where You Step

It was a spring morning in the centre of Bristol at about 4am. Now this little job was about five doors up from the massage parlour where I attended a bomb call about a year earlier. This premises was a grotty little storage facility where they stored the hand-pushed hot dog carts that you used to see around the city in the

70s and 80s. These carts had a Calor gas bottle in the bottom that lit a burner, which provided the heat to cook burgers on a grill on top of the cart. The heater also heated a water container that was home to the frankfurter German sausages sold by these vendors.

These carts could be seen around the city centre outside the Hippodrome, the Hatchet pub in Trenchard Street and all around Broadmead, predominately on a Thursday, Friday and Saturday night, selling hot dogs to late-night revellers.

Down by the Calor gas bottle they had a storage space for the bread rolls. Basically, they were not nice. I never, ever purchased anything from the vendors (they were predominantly undesirables from one particular well-known Bristol criminal family).

In these premises which were allegedly being burgled (you are having a laugh!) were about six or seven of these mobile food carts. There really was not much to search and Major cleared the area in about a minute.

I then turned my attention to the rear yard. As I opened the back door, Major ran ahead of me and I unfortunately followed suit. The concrete yard appeared to be on the same level as the floor of the shop. A big, big mistake!

What appeared to be concrete was in fact the accumulated food debris of days, weeks, months and possibly years gone by, which had been slung out.

At the end of every night, it would appear that the individuals who operated these haute cuisine contraptions would simply sling the water and bits of sausage and stale bread or burgers out into this yard. Over time, this residue built up and up and what was once possibly a twelve-inch step down into the yard now appeared level.

Oh dear! Poor Major and poor me! Before I realised, Major was up to his belly and I was up to my calves in supersonic crud. Our weight had broken through the four-inch crust and we were confronted by the pungent, repulsive, diabolical gunge underneath.

It was like paddling up to your shins in hundred-year-old rotting food. The smell was indescribable. There were no intruders, and it was not a job at all then. There was no alternative – I had to 1) throw my boots, socks and trousers out 2) thoroughly clean the van (as we had to travel back to Bower in it) and 3) thoroughly bath Major because he stank to high heaven. I got home about 8am that morning, instead of 6.30am.

Below are three additional examples of things that I saw as a young officer on patrol in and around the Entertainment Centre in Trenchard and Frogmore Street, concerning mobile food vendors.

1. I saw a trolley overturned, frankfurter sausages splayed all over the pavement covered in hot water, and I saw some sausages picked up, dusted off and resold.
2. I saw an elderly man selling hot dogs whilst chain-smoking. The ash from his cigarettes dangling from his mouth fell into the sausages and was quickly stirred in and recycled – a smoked sausage, perhaps?
3. A lady vendor had reason to argue with a customer. The customer hit her and she grabbed his nose with her metal tongs, causing small cuts either side of his nose. A drunken yob appeared, requested a hot dog, and she removed the tongs from the man's nose (there was a small amount of blood still on the tongs) and served the hot dog! *Bon appétit!*

The Hippodrome Cowboy

Some of these quick little stories have varying amounts of humour attached to them. This one, for example, had an element of fun to it. I was just very glad that the manager of the Hippodrome had a sense of humour.

As with a lot of my adventures, this one occurred at about 2am. We received an A1 (burglar alarm call) to the Bristol Hippodrome, in Bristol city centre. The first units to arrive found that the alarm had activated high in the roof, and upon investigation, an unsecured door out onto the roof was discovered. It was feasible that an intruder was in fact on the premises, hence yours truly and Major were sent for.

Upon our arrival it quickly became apparent what a rambling building the Bristol Hippodrome actually is. It isn't just the auditorium; there are levels above and below that house offices, dressing rooms, storage rooms, prop rooms and so on and so forth. Because of the complex nature of the premises I decided to take the general manager along with me. My reason for doing this was that he knew every nook and cranny in the place. He had been there years and he knew every conceivable hiding place. It was a no-brainer; with him along on the search we wouldn't miss anything.

I instructed all the other bobbies to remain on the outside, covering possible exit points. Plus, we had two PCs out on the roof where the unsecured door had been found. Before commencing our search, I explained to the Hippodrome manager that Major could be quite an aggressive animal. I gave him these two instructions: 1) stay very close to me at all times and 2) don't even look at Major, and under no circumstances stare at him.

We commenced our search from the roof and my theory was that if anyone was in the theatre we would drive them out into the arms of the waiting police. Well, it seemed a good idea at the time. As we climbed endless sets of stairs to our starting point you could not help but notice all of the glossy posters that were displayed on the walls advertising their next big presentation. It was the cowboy musical *Oklahoma!*

Eventually we got to the roof exit, and after a brief word with the two cops out there we started our search. Mr Hippodrome Manager stuck to me like glue. The search seemed to take ages. I honestly never appreciated what a large, intricate and quirky building the Bristol Hippodrome was. There seemed to be staircases everywhere. The auditorium was huge, with three levels and boxes on each level, plus changing rooms and the like. A lot of rooms were quite tiny, in fact. Then there was the stage area and beyond, and all of the prop storage departments; it just seemed to go on and on.

Eventually, after about twenty minutes we were stood at the top of the main entrance stairs that led from the street up to the stalls. Major was descending the stairs in front of us and when he reached the bottom he shot off very quickly to his right, growling loudly. Suddenly we heard Major barking, growling and behaving very aggressively, and in my mind obviously attacking someone.

There were ripping sounds followed by smashing noises, which were emanating from the lower foyer of the theatre. I told the manager to stay very close to me, as I believed Major had located someone or something.

My only concern at this stage was that I had not heard any cries for help and no screams of agonising pain. No shouts of "Get him off!" As we turned the bottom stair into the lower foyer my very bright Maglite torch beam picked up the frightening sight of Major ripping the shit out of a full-size mannequin dressed as an Oklahoma cowboy (which was advertising the forthcoming attraction). Understandably this had toppled over and was being subjected to a truly ferocious assault. Both trouser legs were in tatters, his poor old hat was in shreds and Major was now trying to rip the face. Amusingly, the arm that he had ripped off still had the six-shooter revolver in its hand.

The cost of the damage must have run into hundreds of pounds. Thankfully Mr Hippodrome Manager saw the funny side and no complaint was forthcoming. The end result was that no intruders were found and no evidence of any type of theft was found, and I think the whole job was put down to an unsecured roof door and possibly a windy night.

As I left and was putting Major into the van, Mr Hippodrome Manager commented, "I wouldn't want to get on the wrong side of him!"

How right you were, sir!

Who Was the Fool?

I have included this story for its unique and unusual circumstances. The date I am not sure of but I think it was around summer 1990.

I was still based at Bower Ashton and was on a late turn, about 8.30pm. Just as I was returning to Bower for grub a call went up: "Any unit priority, jumper on the Suspension Bridge, Leigh Woods Side."

I was less than a mile away and although obviously this was not a dog job I immediately responded. A police officer's absolute priority is the preservation of life.

Over the years I had witnessed a few jumpers from the bridge. It is not a nice thing at all. In my limited experience I had found that people who were desperate to end their own lives just did it.

The two previous occurrences that I was slightly involved with were as follows:

The first occurrence was around 1982 or 1983, again on nights; a motorcycle was found abandoned, lying in the road in the centre of the Suspension Bridge. It was obviously very dark and very difficult to see much at all down at road level on the Portway.

After getting the fire brigade up and out of bed the mystery was eventually solved with the aid of their powerful arc lights, when a pair of legs were spotted about twenty yards out into the riverbank (city side). These legs were just sticking out of the mud, as it was low tide. The deceased was a teenage lad who had been jilted, or had had a row with his girlfriend the previous evening. The top half of the body was embedded in the soft mud as the result of impact from the 250-foot fall. What a tragic and senseless loss of life.

The second occurrence was a few years later. This time it was lunchtime. Again this was a young man who apparently, when starting to walk across the bridge from the Clifton side, suddenly climbed up over the railings and was gone. This poor chap landed on the footpath just at the side of the road canopy about 250 yards from Bridge Valley Road. Once again I was on the Portway, returning to Bower for lunch. I was the first officer on the scene and probably there five minutes after he had jumped.

So as I drove along the Clanage and then up Burwalls I was of the hopeful opinion that this might not be a genuine jumper but maybe an attention-seeker, a cry for help or just a drunk needing help.

The other thing that was unusual about this call was that the potential jumper was on the parapet on the Leigh Woods side. There are a few reasons why this is slightly unusual:

Most people contemplating suicide are probably living in the city, and hence would approach the bridge from the Clifton side. The drop from the Clifton side is almost 250 feet, practically as soon as you walk out onto the bridge. The drop from the Leigh Woods side is initially quite small, maybe thirty to forty feet, and then the sides of the Avon Gorge taper away. I would imagine if jumping from the Leigh Woods side, the possibility of a very painful fall (hitting trees, etc.) would deter some folk. A clean jump from the Clifton side would achieve the death wish in a much less traumatic fashion.

As I approached the bridge I saw one of the Clifton Suspension Bridge attendants standing on the stone parapet. I could see that he was talking to a large chap who was stood on the wall of the parapet.

I thought there would definitely be no requirement for my dog at this incident, so I parked a good fifty yards away. I didn't want to upset anyone with the sight of police vehicles or the sound of a dog barking. I got out of the van and walked towards the parapet. I purposely did not wear my flat cap, trying to keep things low-key and non-official.

As I joined the bridge attendant, the guy stood on the wall was hollering things like, "Keep back", "Stay away" and "I will jump, I'm not f*****g about!" He was in quite an agitated state, and I asked him his Christian name and he told me to "f*** off!" Trying to strike up a rapport with this guy was not going to be easy.

I again asked him his name and what all this was about, and in some ways I wished I hadn't bothered. He screamed at me "My name's Andy. Now f*** off." He instantly went on ranting about his missus. Now I don't know if he meant his wife, his girlfriend, his partner or what, but goodness me, was he pissed off with her. She nagged, she moaned, she had no control over her spending. From what he was shouting there were kids involved in the relationship, and this type of bust-up had occurred many times before. He kept on shouting over and over, "I've had enough! She don't think I'll do it, but I'll show her!"

Trying to placate him, I slowly moved closer and closer to him. He wasn't really listening to me at all. I was just the main focus of this guy's ranting. But then something I said made him stop in his tracks. All I said was, "Look, come down, don't be a fool!"

He looked me in the eyes and said with real venom, "What did you say?"

I replied, "Don't be a fool!"

With that he flew off the wall and attacked me like a lunatic! He was fighting, mad, screaming at me, "I'm a f*****g fool, am I?" He was punching and kicking me. He was quite a big fella and his punches and kicks were hurting. We were rolling around the ground and he continued fighting and swearing at me. I had no option but to defend myself, so I started giving back as good as I was receiving.

This ruckus on the ground seemed to go on for about ten minutes, but in reality it was probably a minute or two, because soon another unit responding to the call arrived and Matey Boy was dragged off me.

I had a few minor cuts and bruises but was not too bad. By this time Matey Boy was cuffed and was lying on the ground. I approached him and said, "What the f*** was that all about?"

Believe it or not, he said, "You called me a fool!"

I said, "Yeah, so what?"

He replied, "My surname is Fool and all my life I have been teased and called A FOOL."

Unbelievable! I could have called him a pillock and with my luck his name would have been Albert Pillock!

CPS decided not to charge this vulnerable adult with assaulting a police officer.

Detective Constable Bitten
1983
B Division

With this incident I think I held the record of three officers seeking compensation from the chief constable for injuries sustained by Police Dog Major (three complaints running at the same time was unprecedented). My trips up to the Federation Office were a regular occurrence in those days.

The following story concerns the unfortunate tale of a Detective

Constable from the B Division, my repeated radio messages that he never heard, the subsequent injuries he received courtesy of Major and the damage caused to his civilian clothes.

As per the norm, this was a night shift. The whole incident happened in and around the Bedminster area of the city. This is on the B Division, which was not normally my area of patrol but I can only think that Derek Gardner (B Division handler on my group) must have had a night off. Just after 1am the night B Division CID officer put up a shout that he was following a suspect in a stolen car in the Southville area of the city. I, along with other police units, began to converge on Southville.

Suddenly the radio crackled into life with, "Chase, chase, he's driving like a loony down Greville Street." In good old Bradley Walsh fashion, the chase was on.

What followed for the next ten minutes was a very hairy pursuit all around the front, back and side streets of Southville and Bedminster. Matey Boy driving the stovec really knew the patch, and he was bouncing us around at breakneck speed. I eventually managed to get in behind the officer so I was third in the convoy. We also had a traffic car behind us, plus a couple of B Division incident cars. The adrenaline was flowing; this really was cops and robbers stuff.

It was at this point I said to comms and all listening radio sets, "If this bloke decamps and does a runner stay in your cars, because Major will be loose and chasing him."

This type of scenario was right up Major's street. If everyone complied with my request, then we would certainly nail this guy. As the chase continued in and around Southville two B Division units had the possibly foolish idea of blocking North Street with their two cars parked nose to nose. Well, this sounded a good idea until Matey Boy, on approaching the two-car roadblock, called their bluff and accelerated towards them. Let's play chicken, he thought. Thank goodness the two B Division drivers saw sense and reversed just in time for Matey Boy to burst through, quickly followed by the detective in his plain CID car, me in my dog van, a traffic motor, plus two other B Division motors. This guy meant business and was not going to stop – he obviously had very serious reasons why he did not want to be captured.

It was at this point I said again to Force Control and all Channel 7 units (which should have included the detective in question), "When the car is abandoned, do not get out of your cars on any account." This was the second warning, which was later confirmed by Complaints and Discipline, who listened to the Force Control tapes.

As the chase continued around the back streets of Southville it became apparent that Matey Boy was looking for a suitable location to dump the stovec and do a runner. He would slow down at certain junctions or side roads, as he was sussing out the possibility.

Major had been loose in the front of the van with me from the off. With all of the fast, chaotic driving and swerving Major knew exactly what was in the offering. He was whining, growling and generally psyching himself up for the forthcoming chase.

I knew that as soon as we came to a stop I would reach across, open the passenger door and the bullet would be off. His target would be the only human being running away from us, because everyone else would have heeded my previous two radio transmissions about not getting out of their cars.

After a few more minutes he turned right out of North Street into Langton Park. A shout went up over Channel 7. "It's a dead end, he's doing a runner." This was it! Halleluiah! Langton Park was in fact a dead end, but with a small lane at the top. I could see red brake lights ahead of me, and the villain stopped in the middle of the road. Then the CID car stopped, with me following suit. I reached over, opened the door and the dog was gone.

This was fantastic; my adrenaline was pumping and by the time I got out I just caught sight of Major's ass scooting around the corner at the top of Langton Park into the narrow lane that I now know leads into Greville Street. I was into the lane in about ten seconds. As I glanced ahead of me, I was totally horrified. The lane is about a hundred yards long. This is what I saw: about thirty yards ahead of me, Major was closing in, laser guidance system fixed, seconds away from contact. Fifteen yards in front of Major (to my horror and disappointment) was the B Division detective. He had unfortunately not heard my two radio messages and decided to chase after Matey Boy himself. This was going to be a very painful and expensive mistake. Ten yards in front of the detective was Matey Boy, who was losing ground on Andy. Then the following happened in slow motion:

Major closed in and attacked the detective. This was the first body he came into contact with. It reminded me of a lioness taking down a wildebeest on the Serengeti. The detective hit the deck and was screaming in shock and pain; I could see Matey Boy up ahead, still in the lane. I jumped over the detective and continued running, keeping Matey Boy in sight.

I was yelling, "Major leave, leave, f*****g leave him!" I was now thirty yards from the end of the lane, still yelling at Major, who was now twenty yards behind me, "F*****g leave him, leave him!" Matey Boy was out of the lane, fifty yards ahead of me. Major was not leaving! His jaws were locked on. I had no option but to let the prisoner go. I ran back to the detective and succeeded in releasing him from Major. He was bitten quite badly and his suit was ripped to shreds. It is easy to say that he should have listened to the radio; however, I know how an adrenaline rush can cause someone to react unpredictably.

The aftermath: the bitten detective complained and was looking for compensation for his now *Robinson Crusoe*-style suit and his pain and suffering. Below is an account from the B Division inspector that night, Inspector Paul Stephens.

Major was a true police dog who certainly loved his work; he fitted in really well with the other animals on B Division.

There were two incidents that stick in my mind and regularly feature in my war stories. The first was the incident with a detective who was a relatively recent transfer to B CID from A Group at BR, and on the night in question he was the night cover DC. I don't remember if he was the one who started the incident (I think he was), but there was a chase around the Southville area of B involving him, yourself and at least two divisional cars.

When I joined the back of the queue on North Street, as the column emerged from Greville Street it was like a scene out of Police Academy. You put out a message on the radio to say that when he (the target) eventually stops and if he abandons the car everyone was to stay in their vehicles as you would be "letting the dog run". Just then the target turned into either Langton Park or Merrywood Road, which are dead-end streets, and the chase stopped. As expected, he abandoned his car and you let Major run. Unfortunately, the detective did not follow your instruction and he started to give chase on foot. As he was between Major and the target he felt the full force of Major's bite. Luckily, Major didn't need any treatment from the vet. There wasn't too much sympathy for the detective from my group, who enjoyed a good laugh.

I believe an arrest was made so it all ended well. At least we thought so until the following night when you came to see me to say that the detective had made a complaint about Major and an investigation had started, with the usual report being required from you. You asked if I could confirm that you had made the radio call because obviously you would be in the proverbial if you hadn't. I was happy to oblige and I heard no more of it.

I don't think it was too long afterwards when there was almost an identical incident involving Ray Smith on A Division.

The best story is one that I can only pass on second-hand. On this particular night there was a foot chase in Hartcliffe or Withywood, and the usual high response was generated by those on duty. One of those to respond was PC Gerry Hodge (who should have been down in Bedminster), and when he returned to the station he couldn't wait to repeat what he had seen. Apparently, on his arrival he was greeted by the sight of you wrestling with Major, who had a good hold on the target and was refusing to let go. As I said, he was B Division through and through.

The Hippy Who Really Did Shake

It was a summer evening around about 1983. Some hippy squatter types had been causing problems at a house in Clifton. These were the New Age travellers who went to Inglestone Common and the early Glastonbury events. Some of you may recall the Battle of the Beanfield near Stonehenge in Wiltshire in June 1985.

I only went along because it was quiet and I had had experience at Inglestone Common where the mutant brigade had got a little out of hand. As I turned up there was a gathering of about a dozen oiks, and their leader was a tall, skinny guy with a plaited ponytail and Worzel Gummidge beard.

"Peace, man, peace, why have the pigs brought dogs?" was the cry.

The local bobbies were trying to move the oiks on, but they were professionals when it came to delaying tactics. Matey Boy Gummidge wanted to see my dog, who by now was barking loudly in the van. Mr Gummidge assured all of us (hippies and police) that he could master any dog, and that Major's aggression was a result of my bad handling, and that in fact he (Major) was a pussycat.

I should not have taken the bait, but I did, and to my utter amazement, as I opened the rear van doors, Major, on seeing Mr Gummidge, fell silent. Mr Gummidge was playing a penny whistle with one hand whilst making mystical gestures to Major with his thumb and little finger on the other hand. I was amazed (and embarrassed), the cops were amazed and so were the hippy oiks, who started to applaud Mr Gummidge.

He asked me to get the dog out so that he could see this fine canine specimen at closer quarters. I agreed to take Major out on his lead but Mr Gummidge had to keep well back and not attempt to touch the dog.

I duly took out Major, and for the only time in his life he got out of the van like a baby lamb. No barking, growling or anything. The look on the poor dog's face was one of utter bewilderment.

Major kept turning his head to the side and looking at Mr Gummidge in sheer amazement and confusion. Major was now stood at my side on his lead. Mr Gummidge was about ten feet in front of me, crouched down on his haunches, softly speaking to the dog. I must confess it was an eerie sight, my hound from hell Major being serenaded by a Worzel Gummidge hippy and not an ounce of aggression on display. It did cross my mind that somehow Mr Gummidge had managed to drug my dog into submission.

The cops looking on could not believe it. Mine and Major's street cred were literally going down the pan. The hippies gathered around were smirking at me and taking the piss. Then Mr Gummidge said, "Can I smooth him, officer?" Smooth him? Normally people didn't come within twenty yards of him.

"No," I said, "that's not advisable."

"Oh come on, he looks like a pussycat!" Major, still gooey-eyed, was in cuckoo land, so I thought, sod this.

Checking that I had Major's lead held securely, I rather naughtily gave him the knee trigger to his right shoulder and instantly *whoosh!* Message received and understood. Major went from being a pussycat to the Tasmanian Devil in less than a nanosecond.

With his lips curled back over his gums, his eyes now blazing green and fire coming out of his nostrils, he lunged forward in a concerted attempt to rip Mr Gummidge's throat out. Thank goodness I held onto that lead.

Mr Gummidge went flying backwards with an abject look of terror in his eyes. Horrendous growls and dog snot were flying everywhere. Major was back; he was up on his rear legs belching sulphur. Mr Gummidge was reduced to a nervous, shaking wreck. His supporters, deflated, picked him up and they all shuffled off down the road.

Major was returned to the van, which with him in it, was still rocking and rolling. It certainly was a funny experience, but I was happy to say normal service had been resumed!

Tea and Biscuits With the ACC
Mr Harry Atkinson – Assistant Chief Constable

I think it was in the spring of 1983 that my skipper (Vernon Essex) submitted a report to our ACC Mr Harry Atkinson, highlighting some of my recent dog successes with Major.

As I have said from the very outset, Major was an extraordinary police dog. He truly was top drawer. He was not the best in terms of training exercise finesse, but operationally he was one of the best. As you know, at work Major's reason for existing was to attack and bite. If to achieve this aim he had to track, then he would track. If he had to search, then he would search. He would never track or search and find someone and then bark. No, he would find them and bite them.

He was a dog who always gave 100%. Vernon Essex, my group sergeant, was a man's man. He was a gung-ho and up-and-at-'em type. He appreciated the job Major and I were doing and he recognised that over a period of time he had had some excellent results, such as:

1. The burglar on the school roof in Southmead.
2. Fairfax House – two found in the river.
3. The tobacconist job – seventy thousand cigarettes found and prisoner taken.
4. Sportsman's Club, Eastville – track and arrests.
5. Gardner Haskins – burglary and arrest.
6. Chipping Sodbury – jewellers arrest.
7. Magnum revolver armed robbery job.

All of these outstanding jobs, plus the normal, run-of-the-mill arrests, meant that Vernon was trying to get me some recognition for the effort I had made. The end result was that I had to go and see our ACC, Mr Harry Atkinson, at the then-Force HQ in Old Bridewell for a pat on the back (it doesn't happen very often, and is so much nicer than a bollocking).

In I went to see Mr Atkinson for a nice chat, a cup of tea and two digestive biscuits. Mr Atkinson was a gentleman. He had obviously done a little bit of homework on Major and me because he knew the facts about a couple of recent jobs. He explained that my performance over recent months, although outstanding, did not in his opinion warrant a recommendation for a chief constable's commendation; however, this semi-official pat on the back would be entered on my personal record in HR.

We talked about Major for a little while and the ACC acknowledged that my dog did possess an aggressive streak. One quite alarming and amazing comment that the ACC made was that he was considering seeking Inspector Langley's (dog section officer I/C) view on possibly using Major as a stud dog to breed a litter of potentially outstanding dogs.

He said, "If he's that good, why don't we breed from him?"

At that time, we didn't have a breeding programme but I can imagine Brian Langley having countless sleepless nights with the possibility of multiple little Majors going around biting everyone in sight.

This little visit into the ivory tower at HQ was very pleasant, and if nothing else I always knew where I could get a nice cup of Earl Grey and a McVitie's biscuit if I ever needed one.

He Never Knew What Bit Him

It was a very hot Saturday night at around midnight; I think it was in August and I believe that Bristol City had played Swindon Town down at Ashton Gate earlier that afternoon.

Lots of Swindon fans had remained in town 'on the sauce', and a huge fight occurred at the bottom of Colston Street and the city centre. There was serious public disorder with well over two hundred yobbos fighting. The three or four central officers in attendance in the city centre were simply overwhelmed, and put out multiple 10.9 assistance calls (10.9 is the police parlance for 'officer needing urgent assistance').

All police units made their way as quickly as possible to the junction of the city centre and Colston Street. Upon my arrival there were fighting yobs everywhere. This was not just a post-match football skirmish; this was a mixture of stay-on football yobs having a severe dust-up with the normal Saturday night Bristol idiots who had had too much to drink.

Colston Street was jammed full of young men fighting. As per usual I had Major loose in the cab with me. He was loving it. He was barking non-stop and his spit was all down the passenger window. What with all his barking and the noise of the battle, things were buzzing. It was a hot night and I had my driver's door window wound down about six or seven inches.

As I said, the road was blocked by 'gladiators in combat' everywhere. I could not move forward or back; yobs were all around my van. I could not get out even if I had wanted to. Major was on my shoulder, barking madly at anyone and everyone, when all of a sudden an elbow belonging to a yob who I presume was just pulling his arm back to throw a punch came invitingly in through my open passenger door window. To Major this was like an invitation to dinner. He accepted the invitation in a flash and lurched across the back of me and sank his fangs into the intruding elbow. There was suddenly blood down the inside of my window; the arm was instantly withdrawn, but not before leaving tiny bits of skin and flesh down the glass.

Because there was so much noise going on all around I cannot honestly claim to have heard any additional screams.

The damaged elbow was gone from sight and never seen again. The crowds outside were still preventing me getting out to investigate. I did report the incident later to the A Division inspector; all enquiries at local hospitals proved negative.

Thank God the Villain had Gone
Brunel Video, St George's Road, Hotwells, Bristol
A Division – Early 1979

Back in the 1970s there was a video shop in Bristol in St George's Road, behind the Council House. It was a one-man operation but the guy who owned it was very pro-police and he always did the boys in blue a good deal.

It was a small unit on the first floor, just above a ladies' hairdressers. I can't think for the life of me what the name of the owner was. However, he was a top man, mid-thirties, long hair and with a lot of money.

His pride and joy was a green leather Chesterfield chair, the sort that you would find in a gentleman's club in Mayfair, London.

His office was only small, but you would always find him swivelling around in his beloved Chesterfield.

Now there had been a few break-ins at other video shops in and around the city and on this particular night when his burglar alarm activated I rushed to the scene. Upon my arrival, I found A Division cops both back and front.

The front was OK but around the rear a small toilet window midway between the ground and first floor had been forced and was wide open. Being young, relatively new and very naive I decided to put Major into the premises to search for any intruder. I certainly didn't want the A Division guys getting the prisoner.

With a heave and a ho, I shoved Major in with his command, "Where is he then?" and left him to it. Now I was still very young in my Major experience and I didn't fully appreciate what an aggressive and destructive little tinker he was. In years to come I would learn not to be so gung-ho and exercise more caution. Anyway, Major was in and I was out.

At first we could not hear much. Certainly no barking. However, after a few minutes we detected some growling and gnashing, and some ripping noises followed by more snarling and tearing noises. We had warned the cops at the front not to enter when the keyholder arrived, but to contact us at the rear in order that I could go in first and reclaim the dog.

After about twenty minutes we were summoned to the front. The keyholder had arrived. In the preceding twenty minutes the growling, ripping sounds could still be heard. In my own mind I was reasonably confident that no one was in there because I hadn't heard any screams coming from inside the building.

The keyholder opened up. On climbing the stairs, I found his door had been forced; nothing sophisticated, just a big boot, and the door frame had disintegrated. The owner had followed me up the stairs, and as we entered his offices via the shattered door it was obvious that a very untidy search of his office had taken place. I called out for Major, who quickly appeared with a piece of green leather Chesterfield chair in his mouth. Upon venturing further into the office a scene of catastrophic proportions greeted us. Yes, there were filing cabinets forced open and desk drawers ransacked (no doubt the work of the long-gone burglar); however, what reduced the shop owner to tears was the sight of what was left of his Chesterfield chair. I honestly don't think Mr Burglar had chewed the shit out of the chair. I think there is a strong possibility that it was Major who attacked the chair and disembowelled it.

It was hardly recognisable. A hardwood frame covered in bite marks, dog saliva and some dog blood. Horse hair (the padding) was everywhere, plus green leather in various shreds. The shop owner was inconsolable!

As we left the scene the A Division bobby still on the scene commented, "Thank God the villain had gone or we would have been calling for the dead box!" (The dead box was the coroner's undertaker who attended and removed deceased persons to the mortuary.)

Police Officer Shot in the Face – the Job Major Never Got To Deal With
A Division – 6th April 1983

What a day this way! The day my police colleague Billy Burns was shot in the face by an armed robber and survived.

A team of armed officers and I were going to stake out a Post Office in Easton, Bristol. Information had been received that an armed robbery was going to take place when the weekly cash delivery occurred.

Everyone was in position well before the cash van arrived, and I was strategically placed a few streets away, concealed in a small industrial estate. Well, we waited and waited and then the cash van turned up, duly delivered the cash and then nothing. No robbery, no villain, nothing! We were told to stay in position for a while longer, and then at about 11am we were stood down.

I joined the armed team at the canteen in New Bridewell for a debriefing about the job. All of the guys were still in possession of their firearms, as they had not yet returned them to the force armoury in Old Bridewell. Remember this was 1983, over thirty-two years ago.

We didn't have ARVs readily available. A policeman with a gun ready to go was years away.

As we were sat drinking our tea a 10.9 call came over the A Division radio: "Officer needs urgent assistance – an armed robbery has just occurred in the Lloyds Bank at Bond Street, Bristol." This was about five hundred yards from where we were sitting.

This was amazing – our potential armed robbery had not happened, but now we had a genuine armed bank robbery and two armed and dangerous London villains on the loose. Everyone scrambled towards Bond Street. Things became somewhat chaotic and confused. There were sightings here and sightings there; apparently two black men in a car that had been stolen from the capital a few days earlier. The radio was non-stop with news and updates.

Then we heard, "Officer shot, officer down in the St Werburghs area of the city." Billy Burns, a uniformed bobby from Trinity Road, had cornered the gunman and been shot in the face for his troubles. Thank God he survived, but being shot in the face is not good news.

This fast-moving incident then took off like a whirlwind. Twos and blues were everywhere. A short while later there was another police shootout, in the Downend area, I believe. One robber was nicked and the other escaped, possibly in yet another stolen car.

By now, I was in the Stapleton area of the city when the radio blurted out, "Offender out and running in the grounds of Frenchay Hospital." This was about a mile up the road.

I was quickly in the grounds of the hospital when yet another radio call said, "Armed robber believed to have commandeered a Cow & Gate milk float. Caution: thought to have a hostage!"

I was now at the hospital entrance at Bristol Road/Old Gloucester Road. I was out of the van with Major on his lead. Then all at once I saw a Cow & Gate milk lorry driving towards the hospital exit. I thought, Wow! What a coincidence. The radio said a Cow & Gate milk float, not a lorry. I duly stepped into the road and signalled the driver of the said Cow & Gate lorry to stop, which he did. The cab of the lorry was at quite a height and the driver had his window wound about one third down. I began to speak to the driver but he totally ignored me and stared straight ahead. Once again, I tried speaking to him, but nothing.

Then voices behind me screamed, "Pete, get out of the f*****g way, the shooter is in the lorry." I was then aware of some of the firearm guys that I had been with at the earlier Post Office job positioned in bushes behind me.

With this the lorry slowly pulled away and went out of the hospital towards the M32 motorway.

I honestly didn't realise that the Cow & Gate lorry was in fact the Cow & Gate milk float referred to, and that the armed robber was crouched behind the driver and had a loaded gun pushed into his back. I must have been about six feet away from getting the driver and myself shot. No wonder he kept on ignoring me!

What followed next was probably the longest and slowest motorway chase in police history.

I was joined by another handler, Ray Holmes of Weston-super-Mare's riot fame. We doubled up in my van. Ray drove, leaving me to do the biz if necessary with Major.

There then followed an amazing eighty-odd-mile slow chase up the M4 motorway towards London. There was the Cow & Gate lorry doing about forty-five miles an hour, numerous police patrol cars and quite a few dog vans. Thankfully we were at the front.

The police convoy must have looked mightily impressive as we progressed up the M4 towards Swindon. Patrol cars were zooming ahead of us and firstly clearing and then closing down the motorway. By Leigh Delamere services this convoy had the motorway to itself in every direction.

I don't know how but Malcolm Popperwell, our ACC, joined the convoy and took overall command. Lots of cars and dog vans were stood down, but thankfully we remained the third or fourth vehicle back from the lorry.

It was adrenaline-pumping stuff to see all the junctions closed with armed police at every exit. As we entered Wiltshire, more police were there waiting and it was exciting to see the Thames

Valley Police motorway units armed to the teeth and passing us.

A few times the lorry slowed down, especially where woodland encroached almost right up to the motorway fencing. Was the shooter thinking of doing a runner? He was eventually going to spend over twenty years locked up in prison, so you can understand why he was considering all of his options.

Ray and I were discussing all the scenarios that could play out, and we agreed that if this did turn into a foot chase through woodland then Major was the ideal dog to meet that challenge. Plus, over the years I had thought about how Major was to finally go via the vet's needle. Perhaps going out to a bullet from an armed blagger wouldn't be so bad after all.

Now for the big anticlimax: as we approached Junction 9 for Maidenhead, Mr Popperwell ACC, Avon & Somerset declared, "All Bristol units to stand down", and Thames Valley executed a hard stop and arrest. What a bummer!

Major could have really made a name for himself and for me that day. I was 100% confident that if Mr Armed Blagger had run we would have nailed him.

Thank God Billy Burns was OK. Billy was a born-again Christian and I think that the man upstairs was on his side that day. I joined the God squad in 1989, but that's a whole new story.

Major at St Annes Board Mills, Bristol
The Bite We Never Told Anyone About
B Division – 1979ish

Here are three little stories from St Annes Board Mills in Bristol.

Boxy Bitten

The Board Mills was 151 acres of factory buildings and open land in St Annes. The plant had closed, leaving a skeleton security staff to patrol and keep the place safe.

For about two years we were lucky enough to use it as a training base; because of its size all aspects of dog training (tracking, searching and biting) could be carried out there.

The three security guards we dealt with were Dave Box, Gerry Knight and Len Dudbridge (sadly Len passed away some years back). With Dave, Gerry and Len we had a fantastic liaison. All three were great guys and we on our group had a great association with them. Here are three short Major stories that occurred in 1979.

The first concerns a little bit of unofficial outside quartering (open searching). As the name suggests, St Annes Board Mills was precisely that, a paper mill, and within about four hundred yards of the security office were a huge stack of cardboard bales. These bales were in approximately three-foot squares and the stack was probably between twelve and twenty feet high by two hundred feet in length. We were on nights and Major was a baby and new to the job. I wanted a volunteer to hide in the stacks. Boxy decided that he was the man. So off he went; he climbed the twelve feet up onto the stacks, and he did it quietly.

After a few minutes I got Major out of the van and challenged the area of stacks in the usual manner: "Police here, I have a dog. If you don't come out I will release the dog." There was a thirty-second pause. I then released Major with, "Go on, where is he?" Even at this early stage of his training Major was switched on and knew exactly what was required of him. He zoomed off, yelping and barking as he went. He was down circling the stacks in about a minute with his head up, snorting in the air, trying his damnedest to locate some air scent. I encouraged him constantly: "Good boy, where is he then? Good boy, Mage." Since we were at an early stage of training I shouted out to Dave to show himself, which he did. Upon seeing Boxy, Major went mad and started to bark incessantly.

The dog was up on his back legs; his front paws up against the bales of cardboard. His head was up looking at Boxy and he was going loopy. Dave was geeing him up, clenched fist, threatening the dog. Dave felt very safe – he was twelve feet up. What could go wrong?

All at once Major broke off from the barking and ran off out of sight around the edge of the stack of bales. This was a very early indication to me that Major was a thinking dog, a dog not to be underestimated.

I was confused. Boxy was also confused, and a little concerned. Justifiably so, for about three minutes later Major appeared on the stack of bales at the same height as Boxy. He had noticed a way up onto the stacks from the rear. Oh dear! I knew what was coming next: Major closed in on Dave and bit his leg. These were early days and the wound was not a hospital job; however, Boxy nearly shit himself and screamed and clambered down from the stack, followed by Major, whom I restrained and put the lead on. Dave was a lucky boy – six months later and it would definitely have been a case for A&E.

I never reported this bite. Despite this, Dave got on really well with Major and was one of only a handful of people (outside of the family) that Major would ever allow to pet or smooth him. Boxy remains a good friend to this day, and now I have given him a mention, I hope he buys the book.

Anyone for Skittles?

One night we were in the security office at St Annes and Len Dudbridge said that he had a little gift for Major. He then produced a skittle ball. What are skittle balls made of? I don't know but Len said, "Go on, you b******, have a go at that." They are very hard; I assume they are made from some type of hardwood.

We then started chatting and forgot all about Major, laid out on the floor chewing on the skittle ball. After about half an hour Len exclaimed, "I don't believe it – look!" The skittle ball had been totally demolished. There was a pile of chewed-up skittle ball bits and it had now decreased to the size of a golf ball. Unbelievably, Major did enjoy chewing anything – people, chairs, lampposts, cars, and now we could add skittle balls!

POLAC – Nights at St Annes Board Mills
1982ish – Winter Time

On this particular night I was the only dog handler on duty in Bristol. I think Norman was on in Bath, Mike Shepherd at Staple Hill and possibly Paul Bath in Taunton.

Nevertheless, I was the only dog handler who visited Boxy and the boys out at the Board Mills. I got there at about 1am. Dave, Gerry and Len's cars were parked up in the large garage, as it was a cold, frosty night. I left Major in the van that night, for some peace. The only other vehicle on the whole 151 acres apart from my Ford Escort dog van was their bright red fire engine.

I had been there about twenty minutes when a priority call went up from A Division to the effect that a beat officer had come across a smash-and-grab at a jewellery shop in Broadmead, and that the offenders were being chased on foot. I immediately dashed out to my van. Quick in, reverse and go. *Bang!* I reversed straight into the fire engine.

The B Division supervisory attended the POLAC and said, "Pete, I can't believe it! A hundred and fifty-one acres and there is only one other vehicle around and you hit it. It's also unbelievable that it was a big bright red fire engine, you numpty!"

I agreed.

Black & White Café Raid – You Two Dogs Cover One Exit!
Grosvenor Road, Black & White Café, St Pauls, Bristol
A Division – 1981

I have described some police officers as fearless. Peter Temlett (Weston dogs), Pete Pugsley (Bristol traffic) and Shutty (Bower dogs) spring to mind.

In all my stories, I have been honest in my writings and I can honestly say that yes, I have been scared – in fact, terrified – sometimes. There have been occasions in St Pauls where my back door muscle has worked overtime.

This little story highlights one such event. We were on nights and the powers that be decided to do a drugs raid at 4am. The target was a quaint little local eatery in St Pauls, namely the Black & White Café. This was the epicentre of the St Pauls riot in 1980.

We had four task force units plus Vernon Essex with PD Sacha and me with PD Major. Four task forces meant we had twenty-four coppers. It sounds a lot, doesn't it? Well, it's not a lot when over a hundred snarling, nasty West Indian gentlemen who are very pissed off come charging at you.

I'll never forget the briefing when someone said, "The two dogs will cover our exit." I wanted to know who was going to cover the f*****g dog handlers' exit?

Well, 4am came and the raid, and consequently minor Armageddon, took place. We needed two hundred cops, not twenty. The Black & White Café is like Dr Who's Tardis. How do so many people come out of such a small café? I think we did nick a few and found some drugs, some money and weapons. What we also found were hoards of very unhappy chappies who took great exception to their lucrative business empires being disrupted.

After what seemed like hours and hours the order came to withdraw. Bottles, bricks, stones, milk crates and dustbins were being thrown at us by this large, angry mob of narcotic businessmen.

Task force van's windows were being smashed. This truly was a dangerous and unpleasant situation. It was not the place to get smacked in the head with a brick and go down. Vernon and I were very close with dogs out and fully wound up. I don't need to tell you how tasty Major was, and Sacha was a good, solid, mature dog also. Major was at his fully vamped level (A1). He was on his back legs belching fire; his eyes had turned green ages ago. Woe betide anyone who Major latched on to that night. I don't think I could have got him off in a month of Sundays. His lips were curled back in sheer venom!

From the task force's point of view, their withdrawal went pretty smooth for them. Vernon and I kept the baying crowd back as they limped off with their smashed windscreens and dented wing panels.

Now it was Vern and me, and this is where the involuntary enema nearly kicked in. I will never forget this black chap who was absolutely HUGE. He was about twenty feet from me and he was tossing a glass milk bottle up and down. He would throw the bottle up and then go as if to throw it.

I screamed at him, "If you hit me and I lose control of this loony dog, he will rip your throat out!" Thank God he believed me and melted back into the crowd!

We then somehow managed to get into our vans and retreat. We took a few bricks on the side, but no windows were smashed. It was potentially a very nasty situation. It was only down to Sacha and Major that we all got out unscathed. Was I scared? Yes, I was!

The Straw That Broke the Camel's Back
D Division
Major's Last Job
27th July 1984, Whitfield Road, St George, Bristol
Serious Public Disorder, Police Officer Attacked

Little was I to know that this would in fact be Major's last slice of the action.

This incident occurred on a Sunday afternoon when a large-scale fight occurred in Whitfield Road, St George, Bristol. For the life of me I can't recall what the fight was all about, but I do recall that it involved a lot of men who ended up attacking a lone traffic officer, Pete Pugsley. Now Pete had managed to put out a 10.9 radio shout for urgent assistance (officer under attack), and all available cops were making their way to the scene to help him. For the record I would like to explain that officer Pugsley was a genuine 'top man', similar in many ways to my friend and fellow dog handler (Pete Wally Temlett – of WSM fame). Pete Pugsley was a fearless guy who could really handle himself and reminded me of a street fighter. I remember thinking that if Pete was asking for help then it really must be one hell of a dust-up.

I can recall that as I turned up I saw Pete on the floor fighting with a few guys, one of whom was a giant of a man. Pete had apparently already dispatched quite a few yobs, but now he had his hands full with these Herberts. Other idiots were on the sidelines goading the yobs on to "kill the bill". My first thought was to drive my van into this group and knock them down like skittles, but then knowing my luck I would have ended up killing someone or injuring Pete.

Because I had been given my last warning about Major biting people I made a conscious decision to leave him in the van and assist Pete by myself. I ensured that Major was in the locked passenger side cage, with the sliding cage door slid across, closed and bolted. I must explain, however, that the hole that the bolt dropped into was very worn and the bolt was not a tight fit in the hole.

I got out and rushed to Pete's assistance. I did slam the driver's door of my van closed, but I had left the window unwound due to the very hot weather that day.

It was a bit tasty for a while, with hand-to-hand combat. Compared to Pete I was an amateur; however, luckily more officers soon arrived on the scene and good old plod eventually began to gain the upper hand.

I was now on the ground wrestling with the big guy who had been attacking Pete; to be honest I was feeling quite knackered as this bloke was lashing out whilst effing and blinding at me. He was spitting and snarling at me, and generally being a thoroughly unpleasant chappie!

Then, to my surprise, this big violent man suddenly let out an ear-shattering blood-curdling scream of agonising pain (the like of which I had heard many times before) and I heard a very familiar growling noise coming from alongside me. To my eternal horror I then felt and saw the black fur of my dog, Major. He was stood alongside of me and was feasting on this yobbo's thigh.

Major had escaped from his cage and leapt out of the van's window, and was now attacking the man that was attacking me. It was like he was saying, "Move over, Dad, and let me help you!" It was almost like he knew that this was going to be his swan song, as he really did not want to let go. After a lot of ear-biting and bollock-squeezing on my part, he finally relented and let go. My prisoner was then conveyed by ambulance to Frenchay Hospital.

How did Major escape from the van? This mystery is easily solved. The wire that formed the door of the cage was quite large squares of wire mesh. Major had simply put his muzzle into one of the squares of wire, then lifted it up, freeing the bolt, and by moving his head to the right sharply had in fact flicked the cage door open. Then jumping out of the van was second nature to him.

I should not have been surprised. If you recall from earlier in the book the incident in the Redifussion yard where he instinctively leapt from the fire escape across onto the portacabin roof, that was truly amazing, nigh on unbelievable, so escaping from a dog van was kids' play for Major.

Sadly, this was Major's last operational event. This was now the end of nearly five glorious years with a dog and companion who honestly was beyond compare. My best friend, who would turn out to be irreplaceable.

At this stage I did not fully appreciate how unique and outstanding my Major had been. For the next fourteen years I had a succession of dogs who were in their own way satisfactory and up to the standard expected of a police dog, but were a mere shadow of the legend.

My love for the job was as keen as ever. I always gave 100% but things would never be the same again.

On orders from on high Major died in my arms at Golden Valley Veterinary Hospital on 14th August 1984.

CARRYING ON

That day in August 1984 was dreadful. Major, in superb condition and perfect health, at just six years old, was put to sleep on the orders from on high.

I understood why. Thirty-four bites in less than five years was unacceptable. To say that I was down was a severe understatement. Major had been my best mate for almost five years. The understanding we had was quite extraordinary. He would ride in the van up front with me, sometimes with his head on my shoulder, keeping an ever-watchful eye out for that potential moment when his services might be required.

The mood at home was grim as well. The kids and Linda were all desperately upset. Things would never be the same again.

Well, things do go on and time does help heal the wounds.

I had another fourteen years to work as a dog handler with a variety of different dogs. The stories concerning those adventures will be written in the months and years ahead, and without doubt there will be *More Job, Less Bite!*

MAJOR'S MEMORY LIVES ON
ANECDOTES FROM OTHER POLICE OFFICERS

When I started writing this book, I sent messages out through various online platforms asking former and serving officers for any anecdotes they might have featuring the legend that was Major. Here are some of the responses I received:

Jeff Birkin, retired PC

I worked at Trinity from 1988 to 1996 on foot patrol for the first three years then into A6 and A7 response for five years.

We were in A6 in St Pauls one late shift and had a call to an alarm activation at a carpet/fitters warehouse in Wilson Street, St Pauls.

We arrived just moments after the call and the front door was ajar. There was no one in the street so any intruder might still have been inside.

With my partner we walked in and the little office to the right looked like someone had been searching the drawers. We started to have a look around the building but immediately realised there were too many hiding places amongst all the rolls of carpet standing on their ends. There was no way out other than the fire door at the back and that would force you along the sides of the building to the front again. In short, anyone who was in there was cornered. We called out but if Burglar Bill was there he was in no mood for a chat.

We contacted the control room and you were there ten minutes later in your Escort van. Notably, as you alighted from the vehicle the van continued to rock from side to side as the dog (I think it was Major) tried to tip it over.

As your removed the huge beast from the van and entered the front, with some serious trepidation and concern for who-ever might be inside, I followed as instructed while my partner got the job of waiting out front for the runner if he came round the side. A warning was issued and went unanswered so the dog was let loose.

I then witnessed the most terrifying sight. For absolutely no reason other than sheer animal anger, the dog bit into, lifted up and violently shook a huge roll of underlay like it was a rag doll. Then, seemingly in utter contempt, he spat it out, throwing it across the warehouse. It collided with other rolls of stock and knocked them down like skittles.

When we tried to lift the roll of underlay and put it back it became obvious that this 70kg chew toy that had been so effortlessly tossed aside was not the mere trifle I had expected. Had I known this when I watched it flying through the air, I would have been well out the door before it hit the ground.

I don't think I've ever been so relieved there was no one in the building as I had no doubt this "A1" could have turned into a "sudden death"! As we sat in the car waiting for the beast to be properly caged, I do remember thinking about how the metal surrounding us seemed so insignificant.

Alan George, retired Officer, Traffic Division

Peter is a tenacious, highly motivated person – trustworthy and hard-working. He was without a doubt one of the Avon & Somerset Constabulary's top dog handlers.

I remember when I was attached to the Dog Section (a try-out with a view to joining). I took the easy way, as you know, and went for Traffic in the end – only had one dog to worry about then: Mad Dog Mansell!

During my shifts with Peter Defer was a pup. Pete said to me he wasn't aggressive enough so every time I saw him he made me give him a little slap on his nose with my gloves. It didn't seem to work at first but a year later when I was at a break-in at Stoke Lane Co-op both Pete and Defer turned up and found the scrotes had long gone. We were stood at the till point with Defer. My back was turned away from him and suddenly I had a severe pain in the right cheek – the bastard had bitten me without warning! I swear he was smiling and saying, "That's for slapping me on the nose, you git."

Lawrie Lewis, retired Chief Superintendent

Have you remembered the break at Wyck Beck Road filling station?

We both turn up as they are making off in their car. I've got the lead as we chase them Into Passage Road. With the car still moving one decamps and I'm out after him. The other decamps and you yell that Major is out. I get one, you and Major gets the other but with them cuffed in the car pleading their innocence we can't find any loot. Major wanders around for a piss and the next thing we know he is foot at your feet grinning with a money bag in his mouth which had been flung from the car but neither of us had seen it come out.

I can see the pair of them still but can't remember the names. One used to live in Doncaster Road but had recently moved to Henbury.

Nick Shaw, retired PC

My enduring memory of those times is you shouting, "Shut up, Major." Could be heard over Channel 7 on VHF in the rear yard at AT!

Went to many jobs with you. Saw Ray Smith's trousers torn off by the dog. However, there was one job that sticks in my mind. I am sure it was you and not Vernon Essex.

It was nights. There was a call in Wade Street outside the Salvation Army about a man in a greatcoat acting suspiciously.

I was round the corner on foot and turned up first. A car then pulled up and then you arrived. The man was stood in the doorway and we started to talk to him. He was acting strangely and then suddenly pulled a revolver and pointed it at us. You let Major go and he took him down.

Note from Pete: Would love to take claim for this; however, my good friend Jimbo Watts and his dog Jason were the good guys on this occasion.

Ray Smith, retired Superintendent

To start at the beginning, I think I was a patrol sergeant on Group 1 at Trinity Road or Central on this occasion. We were on nights and went to an alarm call at a tyre depot at Avon Street. While we waited for the key-holder to arrive you threw an old discarded tyre to Major, and he proceeded to chew it up into shreds. That was the first time I saw his awesome jaw strength and complete stupidity (the dog, not you, although you ran him a close second!).

Later on that evening we were called to backup C Division at the tennis club (now called Bristol Central Tennis Club), where there had been an alarm call and report of possible intruders. You and I arrived and I remember Brian Maggs being there because of his later behaviour (laughing). Again, while we waited for the key-holder we decided to put you and Major over the fence, maybe twelve to fifteen feet high, so you could have a look around the outside of the club house. Having completed this, you decided to come back over the fence and lifted Major over first. We helped him over and he lay down to wait for you as you climbed over. I then stupidly decided to clasp my hands together to help you descend the fence. As your big size-12 boot landed in my clasp, it crushed my hands against the fence, causing me to shout some choice words and encourage you to stop crushing me.

Major, hearing the commotion, obviously thought, "Someone is attacking my dad," and launched into an attack on the imagined attacker: me. He landed on the inside of my right thigh, within an inch of my balls. I unclasped my hands, causing the non-skinny you to land on top of me and bring me to the ground underneath you. This again stopped me defending myself as Major continued to wrestle to separate me from my manhood – luckily, unsuccessfully.

Eventually you managed to get to your feet and call him off as I lay there, dazed, clutching my crotch where the remains of my trousers, comprehensively chewed by the dog from Hell, flapped in the wind. All around me sympathetic police officers showed their concern by laughing their heads off, which had also stopped them helping me when I was being severely assaulted.

Eventually Brian Maggs, still laughing, got me into a police car and took me to the BRI, where the doctors and nurses showed their sympathy by behaving just like the police and pissing themselves laughing when they were told the cause of my visit. It didn't help that it had been a false alarm at the club.

They couldn't stitch up the bites due to risk of infection, so I had to go sick for a week and attend every day to get the wounds redressed. I still have the photos somewhere! Luckily I have managed to have three healthy children since that time, and so am grateful that Major's aim was off!

I put in a disability claim to the DHSS at Flowers Hill, Brislington. Eventually an August committee called me for examination and decided that I was going to be assessed as 1% disabled for one year. That amounted to £50, which probably just about covered the petrol costs for my hospital and DHSS visits, so thanks for that.

The other incident. I don't remember why I jumped in the van, but a smash and grab sounds about right. Major, again on the offensive and excited as he tended to be, launched himself through the open front door of his cage and sank his teeth into whatever he thought was again attacking his dad. Fortunately, it happened to be my helmet, which I had not had a chance to remove in our haste. His teeth grabbed it and nearly pulled my head off – luckily, I didn't have a strap on it. He then took it back into his cage and shook it around to kill it while you shouted at him and flailed his lead around to keep him back in his cage and not come forward again to have another go at the perceived attacker in the front passenger seat.

The other incidents I remember about him, although I wasn't there, was him chasing after a fleeing villain along a cycle path – I think in Eastville – and you shouting to everyone to keep still. Although he failed to bite the villain, he satisfied himself by biting someone on a bike coming the other way and/or a policeman.

The next was when he went with you on a bus to deal with a lot of rowdy youths and bit everyone up and down the bus.

The last and most infamous was when you chased a stolen moped two up into a car park at Temple Gate/Redcliffe, where it was abandoned, but not before the passenger got off. Major decided instant justice was in order and bit his leg like he bit mine, but instead of taking a nibble he bit a chunk of flesh out. I believe the charges were reduced against the villain as he was deemed to have suffered sufficiently already.

Graham Voisey, retired Officer

There can't be many who don't remember your famous hound!

Neil Weaver, retired PC

From memory, most of what I recall, which is still fresh in my mind by the way, is not for public consumption!

You always warned us NOT to stare or even look at Major!

Steve Wright, retired Officer

I remember Major – he scared us all and thank God you had the lead. The bit that sticks in my memory bank are the telephone box runs – the 'proby' would get a head start and make for the phone box in Broadmead. Major was then unleashed on the suspicious and terrified proby who had to close him/

herself in the phone box before Major caught up. No casualties recorded but a fab initiation – never done however in the presence of Eric Dinnis or John Clapp!

Then there was the time at Temple Way when your van took off when you off-roaded chasing a the scroat of the night. Major shot out of the van, took a chunk out of the scroat, we all arrived to find blood and fangs, followed by an ambulance and a complaint that went badly for Major.

Many more but I'm not sure if it was another dog and handler. The best of the bunch was a hot night in Small Street in the City, dog handler chases a bad guy involved in a Centre fight. Bad guy runs up an alley followed by handler leaving driver window open, and dog in back with cage door open. Scroat No 2 comes along, sees 'unattended' police van and open window. The thought of pissing on the police came to mind, so he unzips and inserts parts through the window – much to the pleasure of the dog who had been offered an uncooked sausage. Further complaints followed – wish I could remember who that was… Who had Sabre?

ACKNOWLEDGEMENTS

The writing of *A Job with Bite* was probably the easiest part of the whole exercise. Having never before attempted such a task, I have been truly amazed at the amount of work and effort involved in getting one's story, pictures and sketches professionally put into print.

There are a number of persons I need to thank, whose contributions have been greatly appreciated.

Nick Culley – I have jokingly referred to Nick as my PA. He is a very good friend who one day could be a potential Lord Mayor of Chippenham. From website design to business cards and marketing literature, his help and advice from the start has been outstanding. He has been a constant source of practical help and morale-boosting encouragement; truly a top man.

Helen and Rowena at SilverWood Books. Professional and helpful throughout.

Joe and Charlotte (NUFC) and all at Hobbs Reprographics, who have designed and provided such excellent and professional marketing aids.

Debbie Connolly and Bravo Working Dog Rescue – unsung heroes in my book (pun intended).

Jason Shepherd for assistance with sketch drawings, and Rob Staplin for his characture of me and Major.

Dave Hitchings, Ray Smith, Phil Hutchings, Roy Schaffer, Alan George, Paul Stephens, Pete Coombs, Chris Read, Neil Weaver, Lawrie Lewis, Bob Scull, Nick Shaw, Steve Wright, Neil Barnes, Phil Petela, Jim Watts, Bernie Mattock, Jeff Birkin, Cyril Haddy,

Bob Buck 'Willis', and all the other ex-cops who contributed anecdotes to the book.

Richard Francis and the directors of AWW for kindly allowing their premises to be used in the book launch.

Ken Elkes, my literary marketing guru (priceless).

Colin, for advice and guidance.

Sandy Osborne, *Girl Cop* author and friend, for wonderful advice and help.

Andy and Alan and all at the Portwall Tavern for their sponsorship and assistance with the book launch.

Gordon Potter Photography of Pontypridd, south Wales, my official book launch photographer.

My hostesses at the *A Job with Bite* launch party: Leanne, Elle, Beth, Chloe and Rebecca.

Mark Henderson for listening and encouraging.

Elliott Moore, the young IT wizard from AWW who, like Nick, is a top man!

Marie at Wave Virtual PR for her valuable assistance in the early stages.

Zoe Gladstone-Smith for photocopying services.

Sharon, Kate, Rebekah, Tracey, Leanne and all the other ladies at RGH who took the time to read sections of the early manuscripts and give opinions and constructive criticisms.

Janice and Graham from Sheffield, my YPs.

Dave Parnell of P&G Contractors and Lyn Evans at Fairway Support Services – thank you for your friendship and support.

Tony Ashworth – top man in Asia.

Mark Webster of Frutition of Bristol.

My wife, Linda, and our children, Janet, Marie, Laura and Adam, for their help, advice, patience and understanding during the whole process.

And finally, the beast himself – Major. Without you, mate, this book would be pointless. I think that I may have said it in the book but I will say it again: as Tina Turner once sang, you were "Simply the Best!"

GLOSSARY OF POLICE TERMS AND ABBREVIATIONS

A1 – Burglar alarm.

Cast – Searching for a track.

Down – Obedience position; dog lies down and does not move.

FTS – Fail to stop – normally after a road traffic accident.

Going equipped – In possession of housebreaking implements, e.g. torch, jemmy, gloves etc.

HR – Human Resources.

Late turn – 4pm–11pm dog shift, only seven hours (one hour of grooming duty at home). Normal police shift is 2pm–10pm.

Nick – Police station (noun)/to arrest someone (verb).

Nights – 11pm–6am dog shift/10pm–6am normal police shift.

PNC – Police National Computer.

RV – Rendezvous point.

RTA – Road traffic accident.

Section – Police dog section / Mounted section – a specialised unit

Skipper – Police sergeant.

Stay – Remain there, do not move.

SV/Stovec – Stolen vehicle.

Tea leaf – Thief.

Toe rag – Thief/villain.

AJWB web site is at www.ajobwithbite.co.uk

Illustrated talks to groups or organisations are available at "Events" on my website. My talks are where I expand in depth on some of the more interesting events and issues raised in my book.

I truly hope that you have enjoyed your trip with me down memory lane with the beast that was Major.

God bless you all,

Pete

August 2016

To be continued...

Stay!

...in *More Job, Less Bite*.
Read about the prison escapee who was caught by Pete and his dog, the stabbing and near death of police dog Defer, and the Bath jewel thieves caught hiding out on a boat!